CROSSING THE CULTURAL BRIDGES

CROSSING THE CULTURAL BRIDGES

WITH MY AFRICAN WIFE

SOLOMON A. MINTA

Copyright © 2020 by Solomon A. Minta.

All rights reserved. No part of this book may be reproduced in any form or by any electronic or mechanical means, including information storage and retrieval systems, without permission in writing from the publisher, except by reviewers, who may quote brief passages in a review.

ISBN: 978-1-64871-666-9 (Paperback Edition)
ISBN: 978-1-64871-669-0 (Hardcover Edition)
ISBN: 978-1-64871-662-1 (E-book Edition)

Some characters and events in this book are fictitious. Any similarity to real persons, living or dead, is coincidental and not intended by the author.

Book Ordering Information

Phone Number: 347-901-4929 or 347-901-4920
Email: info@globalsummithouse.com
Global Summit House
www.globalsummithouse.com

Printed in the United States of America

Contents

Chapter One 1
Chapter Two 33
Chapter Three 40
Chapter Four 51
Chapter Five 61
Chapter Six 69
Chapter Seven 75
Chapter Eight 85
Chapter Nine 105
Chapter Ten 114
Chapter Eleven 119
Chapter Twelve 131

Chapter One

Despite all the negative stereotypes and scenarios heaped against some foreigners, especially the Africans, I was passionately motivated to date one. I knew my decision would throw a big opposition from my parents and peers, but I could not help it. At that time the only thing I knew about the people from other countries was the negative stereotypes about other people, of which Africans were the main victims.

It all started in my chemistry class where I sat next to an African student during my last year at School. Ironically, we sat together alone in the same row for the whole semester but we never had anything to say to each other even though she was kind of enticing to the eye. Because she was an African I regarded myself as too good to talk to her. I never noticed her for anything for that was what the society had taught us about them. My mental faculties woke me up for some reason and I began to see things differently from other people. I guess it wasn't I alone. One day the entire class went wild when the African student came to the class late, the African outfit she wore was so beautiful that the whole class went wild on her. The guys had a habit to stomp their feet or hit slightly on their desks whenever a best dressed female student entered the class. That was our way of appreciating the beauty of womanhood. Her outfit was sewn to reveal the perfect cleavage of her medium sized breasts and her protruding nipples. It was just too sexy I could not pretend anymore; I just became lustful toward her, but I had to move fast before some of these womanizing guys in the class beat me on this. I was kind of worried about my parents but since I was above eighteen years in age I could work my way around that. My mother can fuss all she likes, I have to make a move to win the heart and soul of this chic, I murmured to myself. From now on I would not want anybody to be calling me mommy's-boy again.

"I have to win her to my side and into my world," I murmured to myself.

"Hi," I said to her when she came to her seat. My greeting was soft and low toned that no one heard me. I was anxious to know how her reply would be. That was my first time of trying to be close to an African. She turned around and looked at me. Her eyes were like a glow of fire that burnt deep into my heart.

"Oh, so now you regard me as a human, a woman per se . . . ?" she responded with an accent. Instantly I felt guilty for my prior conceptions about her until now but I have to grow out of this.

"There is time for everything you know," I said softly to her.

Since that time my mind was dead set. But it would not be that easy for me to cross over that cultural barrier. Sometimes it was just my instinct as I entertained within me that I was too reserved or proud to ask an African for a date. There were just too much defamatory remarks against them in the books and on television screens. But at the same time something within kept telling me to take this adventure before someone else does. So far we have been greeting each other and my eyes follow her wherever she was on campus.

One Thursday afternoon, I went to the new student cafeteria I saw her sitting at the same table with another male student. I was shocked to see her having lunch with a fellow student. She had a medium bowl of fish salad and she asked him if he wanted some salad. She gave half of her salad to him. To my surprise, in addition to her generosity, she was smiling, talking and even made some jokes with this male student. My veins began to stiffen within me when I saw this girl in such a happy mood. Today I decided to swallow my pride and to do whatever I had to do to win her love. I walked to their table to extend my greetings.

"She told me you are in her chemistry class," said the guy.

"That's nice of her . . . she is very special in the class. . . . ," I mumbled softly. Both of them had mixed reactions about me . . . I could see from their looks. She stole a glance at me.

"You might be up to something," said the guy.

"Well, I will see you all later," she said and then left us. Two of us looked at each other. "Man, what did you come here for . . . you fucked up my plans," said the guy.

"I am sorry ... I didn't know about your plans," I said.

Having realized that someone else was interested in her, I began to be more persistent about my obsession toward her. I tried as much as possible to iron out any opposition I would face in my attempt to date the African girl. It would be a difficult task telling my friends about the crush I had on a foreigner. When I finally revealed my intentions to some of them, the responses were sarcastic comments such as: What? Why do you want to date one of those jungle monkeys? I was bombarded with much opposition as my friends attempted to discourage me from getting involved with an African. I defied all of their ill advice and went ahead with my quest to date her.

But one of my biggest challenges was how to stop the nonstop harassment I would receive from my home boy, Mark, who was my main man. I knew for sure that he would use this opportunity to pay me back when I tell him about my intentions about this African chit because I had once scorned him about his intention to date someone. Since then he had vowed to pay me back and consequently we have not been talking for a while. I had to apologize for my actions. Now that we have put the past behind us, at least for now, I knew he would one day find a way to repay me back so I tried to keep my crush for the African from him.

My problem was how to start to make my approaches toward her. If she had been an American sister, it would have been no problem for me. I wished I had an African male friend who had an experience in dating an African sister like her.

One Friday, I had a doctor's appointment so I was to miss that class but I went to the class early in the morning and placed a beautiful card with the words, "*I CHALLENGE YOU FOR A FRIENDSHIP.*" at the spot where she sat. "I wished I could tell someone else about how serious I was in having a crush on an African student and the significance of the card," I contemplated. Throughout that weekend I wished that card would open up a way for me. On Monday, when I came to class, she was already there with my card in her hand. When she saw me, she opened it and stared at it as if she was seeing it for the first time.

"I think this card is from you," she said. Her voice was like an angel. There was a sensational feeling all over my body.

"The card is yours. Someone gave it to you ... ," I said. She put the card back in its green envelope and placed it in her book bag.

"Who is that someone?" she asked.

"I don't know and I don't blame the person either. You are like a queen in this class," I said. "Anybody can give you a love card," I continued. She gave me a strange look. At that time, our chemistry instructor, Mr. Asmara entered the class and the noise quieted down and soon after he started teaching the class with his usual style of asking questions based on the previous lessons. To my surprise, this particular day she participated a lot in class and we all marveled about her smartness when she answered most of the questions that the instructor asked.

Later on, while I was lying in bed, many alternative plans came to my mind. First I thought about contacting one African lady, who worked in the administration building, to discuss my intentions toward my classmate. That would not work because my friends had some confrontations with her before. They called her all kinds of funny names and I contributed to the laughter. I felt bad about it but it's too late now. Then I thought about just assuming her to behave no different from an American sister and just go to her and ask for a date. I looked around my apartment to decide which one of the wall decorations I should replace with something reflecting Africanity. My gaze got stationed on a calendar which I had marked December 24 in red and green marker. The date reminded me of my birth date and the celebrations I had during the previous years. Deep in my mind, I had wanted to stop to celebrate my birth date this year because of the behavior of my girl friend during the last years celebration.

As I continued thinking about the date and my intentions toward this African girl, I finally decided to go ahead to celebrate my birth date and the Christmas Eve together in a grand way. My intention was to use that day to lure the African sister to attend the party through whatever means I could devise. I realized that before I could succeed in my strategy, I had to be able to bar my girlfriend, Yolanda from attending the party.

Even though Yolanda and I are deeply in love with each other in many ways but few of her behaviors are too much for me to bear. She totally blew my devoted love toward her away when one day, out of jealousy, slapped the face a plutonic female friend of mine in public for no apparent reason. The irony was that, this chic, who was sexier than Yolanda, had offered me her body, sex, long before I met Yolanda. She pitied me at that time that I had been going so long without a girlfriend. To her dismay I refused her offers.

Soon after refusing her favor to me, I met Yolanda and I gave her all my love. But now, because her jealous action my love for Yolanda was slowly peeling off from my life while the African girl was coming in to sit in my heart. All my friends and relatives knew that December 24 is my birth date and I never failed to organize a party. For the past two years, a Jewish friend of mine has been celebrating our birthdays together. The Jewish friend and I happened to be born on a Christmas Eve but unfortunately, according to what he told me, his birth is slated as a curse in his family because of his birthday. He told me, "You are just lucky you can celebrate your birthday with joy...," one day when we met at a restaurant to try a new menu on their list that comes with a free T-shirt. "What are you talking about? Birthdays signify joy especially when it falls on a Christmas day," I said. To my surprise he stared at me and I could see his eyes getting wet with droplets of water. For the first time, I felt like crying over someone else's grief.

"What's wrong... Bravasky?" He looked at me and held my right hand.

"My parents regard me as cursed member in the family because I was born on December 25 on a Christmas day." I do not know much about other people's faith but I know that all religions: Judaism, Christianity, Islamism and many other ones originated from the East," he told his story with his face looking sad. I could not deduct any sensible reason for his woes. Why do you let this bother you so much? Wasn't Jesus a Jew?" I asked

"That is the point I find it hard to understand. Instead of my parents to regret what their ancestors did to crucify a righteous man they are crucifying him every day by hating or ignoring anything associated with Christianity." he said.

After our brief conversation we concluded to celebrate our birthdays together so that he could invite his colleagues to enjoy with him and forget about his parents. He came in with his girlfriend, who was carrying his birthday cake, and a few friends. While looking at the calendar I had another alternative plan about the African girl and me. "If I succeed to bring her to my party I would be able to tell her my feelings toward her," I convinced myself.

I wished I could be able to walk her unto the party floor to introduce her as my new girlfriend just like the Jew and his girlfriend. "Time will tell," I murmured to myself.

I lived in the part of the city, where the environment is characterized with a long foliate, running stream, with parkways running parallel along its banks. There are many picnic areas and tables and the air from the foliage fresh water cool water is perfumed with the scents of the wilds. My one room apartment overlooked the section of the part where most activities on the park take place. I assumed she would enjoy it very much when she comes over. It would remind her of her home wild life and the jungles. I would show her a picture of a deer I had taken from my window. For me to bring all my secrets dreams into fruition, I needed the help of my sister.

Even though I wasn't sure whether my dream girl would attend the party, I spent part of my remaining grant money to refurnish my room with a new bedroom and living room sets. I made use of my sister, who does interior decoration as a hobby, to do the Christmas decorations.

While Darlene, was decorating the apartment, I went out for shopping. After going from store to store, about twenty in number, I became exhausted trying to buy something that was a rare commodity at that time. On the third day, I had promised Darlene to bring something to hang on a special place I had reserved on the bedroom wall.

"You might be buying something special for your sweetheart," said Darlene when she saw me removing a picture of Yolanda from the wall.

"What would happen if I bring something that had nothing to do with Yolanda?" I murmured to myself. I had no knowledge of what I have in my imagination to buy but I had an idea of buying a carving from Africa. While I was out shopping, I saw two white females who were waiting for the light to turn green at an intersection. I overheard them talking about an African doll they bought at a store. Luckily they mentioned the name and the location of the store. Before the light turned green for us to cross, I made a U-turn to go toward the direction of the store they just mentioned. Georgetown was a place considered as reserved for the rich. Many people of low-income people don't waste their time to go there. But I had to go there to find Europa and Africana Imports, which I wrote on a note pad I strolled through the streets of Georgetown, I accidentally found the sign "European African Imports (EAI)," after familiarizing myself with so many other stores where the rich guys at campus shopped. I did not waste time to figure out the meaning of the abbreviation. I entered the store and have never been as lonely as I was in this store. There were two sales girls, all assisting other customers.

The person at the cash register, I presume the owner, was just staring at my movements in the store. One of the customers had to go outside briefly, but no one asked to help me. But I had come to the right store so I didn't bother. Prejudice is inherent in the human blood. My people do the same thing to the Africans so why not me. Luckily, I spotted an African doll, carved on a flat wood surface showing female Breasts, hand, face and legs. I lifted it up from its base and looked at the bottom. Made in Ghana–Fertility Doll $55.00. I read. No matter nobody was paying attention to me. They might have thought I was there to steal but after giving the cashier a hundred-dollar bill to pay for the highly priced doll, they felt ashamed. They delayed me in the store for almost twenty minutes, telling me the history and the origin of what I have bought. They took me around to show me many others but it was too late. I liked this one even though I wasn't sure of her nationality. When I came home, I wrote in my dairy: "Today I had tasted discrimination which is an inherent part of human beings."

"I got something . . . something nice and feminine," I said to Darlene when I came home. She stopped what she was doing to have a first look of this special thing I have purchased. "My sister you won't believe what I experienced," I continued.

"What happened . . . ?" she asked.

"I experienced discrimination today."

"Why . . . Georgetown?"

"Well, you know we do not belong there. I was there last time and people gazed at me like I was crazy or something."

"Well, but this thing cost me $55.00."

"What! This ugly thing might cost $5.00 at McBride's."

"Stop that. Look at the bottom for the price." She looked and then questioned me several times why I want to hang something from Africa in my room. Her fear was that I might be bringing some voodoo spirit into my room. I had to let her know on a serious note that we should not be treating Africans like the white folks do to us.

"I think you are in love with an African?" I could not answer her at that moment. I just smiled. I wanted to reveal the secret but I know my sister, she cannot keep secret and she talks a lot. On the other hand, if she doesn't know anything about my crush on this girl, she might embarrass me at the party, knowing how close she and Yolanda had been.

"We will see...," she said and went back to continue her work. Darlene had done a perfect job to get the room ready for the party by December 19, 1977.

Today is the last day of school and I have not succeeded yet to invite her to the party. In the morning before I reached campus, I called Keesha and devised a plan with her. She is one of my female running buddies. She would do anything for me when it concerned me trying to get close to a sister. Keesha was to sit at my seat, making sure she got to class before the African student arrived. Keesha would put my special party-invitation card in her seat. She was also to make sure that she kept the card and not to throw it away. I sat at the other end of the auditorium. Five minutes later, she entered. Her appearance was more attractive than ever before. She wore a gorgeous two-piece multicolored African outfit and her feet fitted in some beautiful homemade leather sandals with some beautiful fabric design. When she entered the class that morning, she caught the attention of everyone. I could see every eye, both males and females staring at her outfit and of course her beauty. When she came to her seat, she stood for a while before noticing the envelope lying at the spot where she would sit. Keesha and I gazed at each other from our locations and giggled. She picked up the envelope and sat. She then turned to Keesha. I stretched my neck high....

"This seat belongs to another person," she said.

"Who is that... she doesn't have a name?" Keesha replied pretentiously.

"That's 'he'...," she rolled her eyes at Keesha. "I don't know his name."

"I am sorry, I didn't know that the place is occupied. I will leave when the person comes." Keesha played it cool and laughed about it.

Moments later, the instructor entered the class wearing a gray turban on his head. He walked as if he had just arrived from his native country. The class became silent. All eyes were turned toward his gray turban fitted perfectly on his head. "These foreigners love their so-called culture," I murmured to my self. Before the professor began lecturing, Keesha excused herself and went to the other end of the class where there was an empty seat. While Keesha was away from her, I kept watching her closely. She looked across the room, from corner to corner as if she was looking for me. I thought the professor realized something differently about her today. He walked over to her and mumbled something in hers ears. She rolled her fingers in her hair and shook her head sideways.

I remained at my new seat until the class ended. Leaving the auditorium, I saw her rushing through the crowd, twisting her blue book-bag as if she was late for her next class.

"You dropped something," a student, behind her noticed.

"That's an invitation . . . you can have it," she said to the student. At that instant my intestines twined within me. ". . . Am I a failure? I contemplated.

"No thank you; I don't go to African-parties," the student said.

"I don't go to American parties either," she said and pushed the card inside her book bag. I became confused, debating within me whether or not she would honor the invitation.

That never deterred me from my plans. I invited only a select few: couples, instructors, family members and close decent schoolmates. I had heard that African women generally don't smoke so I wrote 'No Smoking' in the invitation cards.

A week before the party, my mother informed me about a dream she had the previous night. Our parents' generation knew very little about the African people, so she narrated her dream like it was a humorous fairly-tale. There was a tall chair standing in our balcony. For some reason it's so old that nobody sits on it yet but my parents won't discard it from the porch. But today my mother decided to sit in it to narrate her dream to me. According to her dream, she saw me sitting on a tall chair and an African woman was standing by my side. She grinned.

"Mom, what is funny about that?" I asked my mother. "You are just like dad"

"Yes . . . ,' she said. She was such an ugly human being, with all the primitive stuff around her neck. " I thought deeply about my mother's dream and compared it to Dora but my mind was made up and nothing could deter me from that. I prayed that my mother's dream would be rather manifested between Dora and me irrespective of my parents' objection. Thanks to the laws of the land, at my age, no parent can stand in the way against my wishes.

"I hope you don't bring any African to this home." To my surprise, she pulled out Yolanda's picture from her purse. She flashed it out in front of my face. I could feel the first time Yolanda and I made love that was the same day she took that picture and promised to give it to my mother. "Concentrate on Yolanda, and be prepared to get married to her. She is a good girl," concluded my mother. But I can't tell the reason behind her advice now because she never showed any interest when I was dating Yolanda.

I left my parents' home with mixed feelings. I told nobody about my plans and proceeded with my arrangements for the party.

One evening when my homeboy, Mark, came over and saw the doll, on the wall he laughed. I just moved away from him knowing how sarcastic he could be about anything African. He followed me with his usual notorious behavior. I recalled the day I made fun about his intention to date a girl we met at a gas station. He bragged about that girl's good-looks over my former girl friend but when I discovered that his new found friend worked at a funeral home. I ridiculed him about it. He could not withstand my sarcastic remark about her. Since then, our friendship never became the same until now. So everything he said I began to think that he wanted to pay me back for the past. But I am not going to allow him to mess up my plan in anyway. I watched him closely about what he did or said.

"Man, what is that ugly thing in your room? What have you been smoking? I am going to stop coming over here; Are you into that African voodoo stuff?" He kept on whining. Somehow I found the courage not to react to whatever Mark said about the doll. My mind was already made up and I did not need his opinion or comments. Nothing could persuade me from the fact that I wanted to get closer to an African chic. Whatever would be the obstacle, I would endeavor to win her love, even though I was scared of my parent's opposition, especially my mother. My dad is pretty much laid back sometimes. Even though dad was very easy going, I decided not to invite my parents this time. I knew that my father loved to give long funny speeches at my parties, expressing his happiness over my academic achievements. I didn't think I was prepared to deal with that this year.

It was about eight o'clock in the evening of December 24, 1977 when the guests began to arrive. My sister and other friends took it upon themselves to welcome them. I wanted to make sure, when she comes, I would be at the door to escort her to a special seat I had for her. At 9:30 p.m. a car stopped in front of my apartment. The driver was wearing some African outfit. That disturbed me. "So all my dreams had been washed down the drain," I said to myself. "Is she coming with a husband or boyfriend?" I stood motionless, wondering in my imagination while another gentleman alighted from the back seat. When I saw the scene, I nearly felt unconscious but I had to hold my composure. She took the invitation card from her leather bag and verified for the address before the driver drove away. She and the other gentleman walked toward us. I was feeling heavy when she came closer to me.

"Oh! You are here too . . . I was also invited," she said, while staring at me with awe.

"You are welcome . . . ," I said. I shook her hand which felt as soft as the cotton wool.

"May I see the hostess first?" she asked, I hesitated for a while and looked around me. I was careful not to say anything that would have made her to leave.

"You mean the girl who gave you . . . ?"

Before I could finish my statement, Keesha and her boyfriend appeared. I had already mentioned her casually to Keesha after warning her not to mention it to Mark and Yolanda.

Keesha, who already knew my intentions, welcomed her with her usual hospitable manners.

"By the way I am the host," I said. She turned around and said something to the guy she came with. I prayed silently within me for her not to turn her back on me. The guy said something to her in their dialect and then she moved a step toward me.

"I am Akosua Dora, in case you forgot my name and (she turns to the guy with her) this is my brother; you can call him Emma." I happily shook their hands while I was introducing myself.

"I am glad he is a brother to her . . . ," I mimicked with smiles.

"Thank you for coming . . . , feel free to socialize and enjoy the occasion," I said.

"You just tricked me to bring me here," she said with a pretty smile. That smile went deep within me and aroused all my human instincts. I walked them inside to their reserved seats.

For the meantime, while the guests were still arriving, I stood quietly and observed her mood swings. As she and Emma, engaged in a conversation, both of them observed everything that was going on in the room. A friend of Keesha, who attended the party without invitation, held a nine-inch smoking pipe. I could see her frowning and she alerted her brother about the pipes. I moved quickly to the brother.

I am sorry. Don't be offended for this gathering is smoke-free," I said to him politely. He accorded immediately and without hesitation he took the pipes away.

By 11:30 p.m., the place was crowded. Dora sat quietly with her brother, conversing in their dialect. At one time, I saw both of them looking serious.

"Africans don't come to places like this. It's unsafe to be among these people," said Emma, who stopped talking when he saw me coming toward them.

"When you are with me . . . you are in good hands," she said.

My fears subsided when I saw Darlene asking her brother for a dance. Darlene, I trusted my sister because she is just a sexy dancer who can mesmerize men on the dancing floor. Both of them danced for a long time. He forgot that he wanted to go home as he was occupied with many females who wanted to dance with him.

This is the time my friends nearly messed me up. Luckily, Darlene had begun to like Dora so she defended me. She acted as if she was in a witness stand before a judge. Everyone was curious to know if my girlfriend, Yolanda, was coming to the party. The incident reminded me of a man playing the lottery whose sole aim was to win. My main intention was to get a lustful attention from Dora, my special African friend.

It was the hardest decision I ever had to make, to break away from Yolanda, my sweetheart for two years. I could not actually tell her myself but it was planned so well that it was she who broke off the relationship. I knew her weakness and that was what I played on. She loved sex, more than any woman I knew and it was like I was the only man that could satisfy her. I gave in to her sex urges without remorse. One thing I knew was that we were so sexually comparable that both of us thought we could never part from each other. But since I made up my mind over Dora, I stopped being intimate with her again. That was enough for her to cheat on me. That was enough excuse to send her away from me without bothering to dish out the true facts. She was furious when I refused to answer her pleas. Her anger knew no bounds. She decided she would get even with me for failing to return her calls. She would constantly harass my sister about my behavior. My sister always knew what was up so she paid her no mind and always gave excuses for me. She would come home to tell me what was going on in Yolanda's mind. That gave me an incentive to continue doing the very things that she was complaining about. One Friday afternoon; I had just left the office and as I was about to enter my car, Yolanda drove up and confronted me.

"I can't believe this. Two years of my life, I have been good to you and you do this to me. You don't even care to know what has become of me. Yea, you must think that I am stupid. I heard about you and your jungle connection." I had never felt guilty like this before.

I wondered how she knew about Dora. Keesha, had to be the one to tell Yolanda about my secret lust for Dora. How else would she know? I began to think how I would deal with Keesha for daring to betray me. I smiled as I thought of the many ways I could use to get back at her. Yolanda thought I was ridiculing her and proceeded to utter a barrage of colorful language about Dora. My anger knew no limit as I heard her begin to abuse Dora, the woman of my dreams. I knew then that all was over between Yolanda and me. That was why Yolanda was not invited to this party. My friends could guess all they want my mind is dead set on Dora.

Luckily, Dora felt free to dance with me. I made sure nobody else danced with her. I whispered several times into her ears, praising her beauty and cool attitude. Before long I made my first bold move.

"Let me show you something," I said. To my surprise she did not object to my request. I took her to the patio and gazed at the cloudless sky. The moonlight shone brightly everywhere on the garden, giving it a magical glow. The sound of the crickets from the bushes, the cool air from the trees and for a bonus to our curiosity a deer popped up from the woods. Dora became excited to see the deer.

"Look!" she pointed. "You have these animals here?"

"They are everywhere. They live along the creek." The appearance of the animal opened up many doors. We were lost in our thoughts as we stood with our eyes fixed on each other, waiting for the next move and turned back.

"I can't fail in this my first attempt; That would be over for both of us," I murmured to myself. I wanted to tell her something, about how much I admire her but it wasn't easy for me to say. She suspected something.

"Why did you bring me here?" she asked. She looked at me with a puzzled-look on her face. There was room now for me to initiate a conversation. I began to think of the right word to say, something that would not anger her.

"None of my parents understand anything about chemistry. I am the only one, in the family, with a college education" I tried to adhere to her question.

"Where are your parents ... I mean your girlfriend?" she asked with a soft voice.

"I don't have any. I am still looking ... ," I said.

"You might be something else. Anyway that picture in your living room resembles one of my cousins. Whose picture is it?" she asked. "That's a picture of me. It was taken years ago." "Come on, sister, I am not trying to hear all of that," I murmured to myself. I took in a deep breath and then looked straight into her eyes.

"This is my own place. I'm twenty-five years old, I don't have to depend on my parents anymore." She looked at me as if she was examining my physical body.

"You don't depend on your parents ... ?" She wondered. I could feel the cultural divide here. I don't know anything about the African culture but once I have started there was no need to go back.

"I was twenty-one when I took that picture." She never said anything again about the picture. As I held her hands she lifted up her head and looked calmly at me. It was as if I could see my image in her glassy eyes.

"I see, that's impressive ... but ... ," she said

"But what?" I asked.

"I really love this place, You might be rich ... ," she said in a seductive voice. "Especially, the scenery ... the deer...."

"I am not rich," I replied with laughter. "I am just a student like you, surviving on the grant money. My parents had taught me how to manage my finances and to use it wisely." The music wafted out onto the patio as someone opened the door. We walked back inside and melted into each other's arms on the dance floor. She was polite enough to dance to some slow music with me. Instantly she aroused my instincts within me, when she pressed her chest close to mine. I could even feel her nipples attempting to penetrate my skin. It was a sensational experience that I will never forget. I could not wait to tell her my true feelings. I knew that I wanted more than conversation. Suddenly, the room filled to its capacity and the air was stifling. We walked outside to the porch to get some fresh air again. Unfortunately, the porch was crowded. Some of my buddies, who have been observing us with impunity, started to make some sarcastic gestures about her. I did not want her to know what was going on. We walked back inside. Darlene was encouraging the guests to eat and drink.

She came and took Dora to the kitchen where her brother, Emmanuel was already eating and socializing himself with the people he had danced with.

"What are you eating?" she asked her brother.

"Just chicken?" he replied. I was very close to her observing her every mood. One of our instructors came over to me and whispered in my ears. "It seemed that you are not of yourself this year. This is your party. You need to pay attention to everybody." Dora caught the drift. She was trying to get some turkey meat but somehow the knife fell from her hand. She turned around and glanced at me.

"... I will eat later" she said to my sister. She and her brother went to their seats and started talking in their dialect again. The guys who heard them talking laughed at them but they never realized that they were laughing at them. To my surprise I caught Emmanuel looking at his watch.

"No! You guys are not going anywhere until..." I murmured to myself. Darlene concluded that the African student was in love with me but she could not show it. "Perhaps, that's typical of foreigners... not as sharp and plain like the American women."

"All is well... this is a special case," I patted Darlene's shoulder. I requested the DJ to play the Gladys Knights' number "Midnight Train to Georgia." The floor was crowded. Everyone wanted to dance to that tune and the most exciting thing was that everyone sang the song and danced at the same time. I was caught up in euphoria. I grasped her and moved some steps with her and then slipped outside with her for a brief moment while everyone was on the floor singing and dancing with Gladys Knight. We walked outside into the open fresh air. I smelt perfectly well, the sweet aroma from her body.

"I think you have something in your mind. You know I am an African; you can't deceive me in anyway." I held on unto her both hands.

"I'm really interested in you and I want to get to know you better," I said. She stared at me. I rubbed my chest to feel my heart beat.

"What do you mean...?" she asked.

"You know it already," I replied. "You just said it."

"I have not said anything," she said. I became confused, wondering why she needed to pretend at this moment. It would be very disappointing for her to reject my proposition. The guests may be laughing at me, and besides I may not get another chance to get closer to her.

"You know what I mean. I would have told you this long before now. I just didn't have the courage to do so. Even a while ago, the deer that visited us came to tell you what I think of you." She took some steps away from me. I followed her. She turned around and shook her head.

"Are you a story teller?"

"No but the truth is that my heart is burning for you with love. You are like an angelic flower sitting in my heart."

"You don't even know me. How can you love me so much? We have just met." I didn't know what to say next. I talked about many things, such as the beauty of the moonlight, the trees, the flowery fences in the neighborhood. It was as if I was looking out of my mind while she was gazing at me.

"For two semesters, my heart had been yearning for you but I was too afraid to cross the cultural barrier. At the time I was trying to show my interest in you, you did not pay me any attention." I said. She smiled at me without saying a word. I became a bit relieved with her smile. I took the opportunity and wrote my phone number on a piece of paper and gave it to her.

"Give me some time also to like you. To like or not to like, to love or not to love, or whatever the situation might be it's a two-way street and never a one-way lane," she said calmly as if she was reciting a poem to me, while accepting the piece of paper with my phone number. These were some of the challenges in dating a foreigner. They seem to be entirely different from us in their perceptions and decision-making strategies about relationships. One of my pitfalls was getting used to these adaptations, which is entirely different from the American dating game.

"I am still wondering why you look like a cousin of mine," she said. I closed my eyes on her remark and pretended like I did not hear what she said. It wasn't a good feeling, especially to me, when Africans say that Blacks in America look like some of their people at home. I hid my displeasure about her comment and both of us amicably walked inside to join the crowd. At this time my friends were contemplating that I was wasting my time to try to woo a jungle monkey. The time was way past midnight but Dora was still with me. At least it was a good sign for me. Darlene brought her homemade bread and bragged that she made the bread.

Darlene took the opportunity to introduce herself to Dora. It seemed that Dora was interested in Darlene's hairstyle. She kept looking at her. Darlene got the message and offered to do her hair for free if she visited her salon with a paying customer.

"You did a good thing for coming. Your coming has opened up our eyes to see the other side of our people. Don't let this be the last time . . . please," said Darlene

"Thank you, that's very nice of you. Nice to know that you're a beautician," said Dora.

"My Salon is at the corner of U and 16th Streets, not far from Woodrow Wilson Senior Living center, near the Park," said Darlene.

"Oh, I know where it is. I pass by the place very often . . . ," said her brother.

"Excuse me . . . please we have to go . . . " said Emmanuel. Dora informed me that they had to attend another function. She politely asked for permission to leave. As if my sister knew my mind; she took Emmanuel inside. I had a brief moment with Dora. And I took the opportunity to give her a kiss on the cheek. I had an inner joy because she was polite about it. I promised to give her a call.

"Your sister is nice," she said. "Your people are too nice beyond my expectation. She said this without commenting on my request to give her a call.

"Unless you live and mingle with people, you will never know or understand them," I said. "Perhaps, if you and I continue like this, we will one day effect a change. . . ." She just smiled and I could see her dimples all on her face. I had wanted to give her a warm hug to let her know that I really liked her personality but Darlene and Emmanuel entered the scene and saw us standing so close to each other. She changed her mood instantly and went to stand by her brother.

"We can go now," she said. "My aunt will be here soon to give us a ride." Emma then turned to me and thanked me and my sister for inviting them for it was a great lesson for me to be among Black Americans.

"We have to go to another function now . . . ," said Dora.

"Thank you all for coming and don't let this be the last time. Remember to go to my sister's salon," I said.

"Don't worry about that. That is taken care of . . . ," intervened my sister.

As soon as she said that a car, a blue Pontiac, came by. The driver, a middle-aged lady called for them.

"Let's go. What are you doing in this neighborhood?" the lady asked. Dora did not answer her. They went inside the car and she drove off. I wondered if I would ever see her again because of the lady's attitude. For some reason my own sister and other girls made fun of the whole situation that I wanted that African girl but she has gone back to the jungles. One of the girls was a good joker; I had to laugh at her jokes.

If you want to see that African girl again you will need to go and find the white man called Tarzan to arrange for you to see her. Irrespective of what they said about her my mind was set on Dora. I paid no heed to what they were grumbling about.

I wonder how someone, in his right mind, would like to date a native of the jungles," said Rick, a friend of mine who had been constantly advising me to date one of the girls in our class. No one could sway me to change my mind. I was just determined to get Dora. After the party I waited every hour expecting to get my first call from her. On the third day my sister joked.

"Is there a difference between an African booty and American booty?" she laughed at me.

"It might be all the same, sister," I joked with her when I found out that she was under the influence of alcohol. Darlene and I sat for a while and talked about many things, such as some frictions between her and our mother.

Five days later, while I was lying in bed, the telephone rang. The caller hung up before I reached the phone. There was no way I could find out who had called so I sat down hoping that it was Dora and she would probably call back again. Five hours later--since I received no calls--I dressed to go out. Just before I left the place, the phone rang again. My intestines began twining within me. I walked to the phone and refused to pick it up at the third ring. I was compelled to pick it up at the fourth ring before the caller hung up the phone. "It could be Dora," I murmured to myself before answering the phone.

"Hello! This is Jason."

"Why do you seem to like me that much? You are a nice guy and I see all of the other girls are checking you out," said the voice on the other line. I assumed that it was Dora's voice because of the accent. I hesitated to answer her because she seemed to have a harsh tone. She did not respond to my greetings but rather bombarded me with a question.

"Perhaps that's the way with Africans," I convinced myself.

"I... I'm crazy about you. There is something about you which I can't explain... Dora. You appear to me like Aphrodite, the beautiful goddess, I can't keep my eyes from off you."

"You don't even know where I came from nor do you know anything about my culture. Don't equate me with the characters in the Greek storybooks. We don't do that in Africa," she said. "How many of your people or my people have you seen relating to each other like what you have in your mind?"

"Well I don't know how other people think. What I know is that you are deeply in my mind on an hourly, daily and weekly basis," I said.

"Well, I called you because you told me to do so. If anything at all, we can be friends... just for the hospitality you showed me at your party."

Half loaf is better than nothing. Now that I have another chance for conversation, I planted joy in my heart.

"Okay, that's fine with me." I replied but the phone signaled with the dial tone. "We did not even say goodbye to each another. What does that mean? I wondered within me.

Since then I have been watching my calendar on the wall marking how many days it will take us to talk again. Now it's two days before the new year and I am still yearning for her call.

Two weeks after Christmas, I had just entered the main administrative building to check my accounts. To my surprise I saw Keesha and Dora chatting just in front of the elevator.

"Look...," Dora pointed to me.

"Wonders will never end, and we were just talking about you and your party." A good feeling of sensation rummaged through me. I shook hands with them with my usual smile. The elevator came down and Dora wanted to part from us. Hey girl... where are you going? You are in America now and must behave like an American," said Keesha, She whispered something in her ears. She laughed and pushed Keesha away from her.

"A bad girl... I am African you know," said Dora. I went over and gave her a kiss on the cheek. Keesha quickly moved away from us.

"I am glad to see you again," I said.

"I am always there. I have not gone anywhere," she said. "Your girl friend Keesha is something else. She is very bad."

"Anyway she is not my girlfriend. What did she tell you?" I asked.

"It's women's talk. You don't need to know." She looked at me from the top to the bottom. "What do you see in me at all?" She asked while staring in my face.

"I can't tell but you are just different from anybody else I have known." Your black silky skin appeals to me."

"Do you know what happened at the party?" "She changed the topic.

"What party . . . ?" I asked.

Instantly her brother appeared and he attempted to pull her away. Luckily she rescinded his attitude, with an explanation that she had not finished talking with me.

"I mean the party we attended after we left your place," she continued.

"What happened?" I asked. She pointed to her brother.

"My brother told my people that I took him to an Afro American party."

"Why? There was nothing wrong with that. I presume he enjoyed himself."

"I know that . . . he enjoyed the party, anyway, much more than I did. But for some reason my people are very skeptical about having anything to do with your people. I was scolded for that."

"Why is that? You are a grown woman. You are not a child anymore."

"You see the difference. You can't talk like this in any African home . . . "

I took the opportunity to explain how we have been deprived of our African heritage but eventually we will overcome our ignorance to be able to embrace our roots, probably in less than five decades

"You are very intelligent," she said.

"Oh thank you . . . did you believe what your people said about us?"

"In a way . . . but I defended you; you are too intelligent to do anything like that."

"Like what?"

"I can't tell you everything; I will see you later." She then left me to join her brother. This time I didn't hesitate to get her number after she instructed me when to call her. We continued to react with each other in this manner till our final days at school.

With persistence and patience she finally gave in to my demands. She did not refuse my dating requests anymore. Within a short time I proved myself to her expectations and she paid me dearly with her nakedness. Once we reached this level in our relationship, our conversation focused on the future expectations. She spoke to me about her culture and her views on marriage and our relationship. I learnt a great deal about her. As she spoke, she was captivated by the music. I knew I would get her regardless of the price I had to pay for loving her.

For some reason, Dora always had some kind of reservation for our relationship. She has been asking me how I managed to be born with a gray patch of hair, about one-half -inch in diameter just above my forehead.

"There are people in my hometown who have this kind of hair. This is hereditary you know," Dora told me this one day after she had come home from work.

"What has that got to do with anything? I don't know where I got it from and don't even worry about that," I just said anything to stop her from saying anything about her people back home. To me I do not care but I hope my people would not raise this question again when they see you.

"In my tribe anybody born with this kind of gray hair is called by a certain name which I won't tell you." I hope you are not one of them," Dora said as a joke.

"Whatever you say is okay with me as long as you continue to be there for me."

One day when I went to pick her up to attend a function at their embassy, she was gorgeously dressed as if she was going to a prom. I was dumbfounded about her outfit gorgeous appearance.

"Damn! Girl! You are so beautiful, I wish I was here before you dressed." She looked at me and rolled her eyes. "Are we going to a prom?"

No but it's more than a prom. After today you will know more about my people," she then patted me on my shoulder.

Twenty minutes later, I found myself among many Africans waiting patiently to enter their embassy building at Meridian Hill. It was like my ears were on vacation. I could not understand anything that was spoken around me. Dressed in designer jeans and T-shirt, I followed Dora to the second floor, where the function took place.

It was the first time I visited any Embassy-to witness what it was like to see Africans in a party I was so proud of being in company with this beautiful African lady. But my pride died within me as soon as I entered the hall which was beautifully decorated for the function. I was lost in my imaginations- seeing the beautiful colorful clothes the people wore. Everybody was well dressed like they were at a prom. It wasn't easy to comprehend some of the men wore big sheets of African fabrics worn over their shoulders. They moved with pride while I was debating within me.

"What're your men wearing... bed sheets?" I asked Dora. She refused to answer me. I looked around but could I not find a brother nor a fellow American brother or sister from here to chat about what was going on.

Dora was just too busy doing everything else and almost shook hands with anybody she saw. The more the people entered, the more I found myself not dressed enough for the occasion.

"We have to go back home because I am not well dressed for this function." I said.

"We don't have to. You will be okay ... until next time." I could not understand her after several pleadings so I had to stay feeling so embarrassed to among such beautiful bodies moving around me. Never did I think that Africans could command such a beauty. My stereotype about them associated with the jungle or whatever we have been calling them evicted from my mentality.

"Next time, please realize that the Africans are always proud of what they wear." Like a parrot, she spoke her language without ceasing that I could not even remember she ever introduced me to anybody. Few people came to me and asked me about our school. "I hope she never portrayed me as a mere schoolmate ... ," I murmured to myself.

The occasion formally started when the Ambassador arrived. Immediately, drum beats echoed from the corner while everybody remained silent. It was like the ancestors chanting through the drum, the music, the melodies and the stories of the oppressed seemed to come from behind the hive; I was overwhelmed. Dora came and stood by me and we held our hands tightly together. "Now I know who you are," I whispered into her ears. "I have heard about African drumming but I didn't perceive it like this ... very real and touchy."

After the drumming the Ambassador gave a short speech highlighting the significance of the occasion. Immediately after that, the dancing started. I could not move from my seat. I really felt underdressed. It was my first time ever of being at a place with no other nationality but Africans. I chose not to dance but I enjoyed seeing Dora in such high spirits. Dora enjoyed herself. We came home at about three o'clock in the morning.

"I am all yours now. You can do whatever you want," she said while she was undressing herself. I was not in the mood at this time. Usually when she talks like that, it's usually a signal that she was feeling horny. She came over to me and placed her hands between my thighs. I stared at her.

"Why are you looking at me like that? You want to change on me . . . ?" she doubted me.

"Oh no!" I said and started rubbing her back. She then read my mind instantly and started to console me. She apologized for failing to tell me the dress code. I could not be too harsh on her because of our cultural differences. We just had to cope with each other. I regard love or relationship as a game with no referees or winners.

"You saw how we were dancing indiscriminately? Next time you can dance with any woman without my permission. That's the way of the African peoples."

"Thanks for all that. I am all right now," I said.

Since then our relationship had improved and we were so compatible that my close friends and relations worried that she might have put some voodoo on me. They could see a big difference in me between the time I was dating other girls and now. I could not explain to my parents how special Dora was to me. There was something different about her which I could not find the right words to describe. The only problem I had was when I was around her people. I could not comprehend their behavior and their negative attitude toward Black Americans.

Thank God. I was not born into an environment of such a strict culture. My parents hardly resisted when I approached them to announce my intention to marry the African girl, even though they had their initial doubts.

". . . is that what you want, an African lady? With all the stuff you see on television?" my mother had said when I first mentioned anything about Dora to her. I had made sure she was alone before approaching her so that my brothers and sisters, who hated the idea of me dating an African, would not have any opportunity to make fun of me. The stereotypical views about Africans were awful and had it not been for the fact that I had intended going to Africa with her after marriage, I would have changed my mind. I looked at my mother and smiled. She turned her eyes away from me and then turned back to me again with a frown.

"But the girl is beautiful and different from these girls over here. She never argues with me about anything," I kept on talking. She wasted no time to register her point of view.

"... because she is afraid of you ... and love can never function in a fearful environment," said my mother. I wondered what she meant by that. Probably I did not need to dig into her mind set. My father did not share her views and instead he supported me and gave me his blessing.

"Somebody needs to set an example for others to follow," said my father. "It's always good to try something new. They know no better; possibly, you will be able to civilize them when you go over there some day."

"Whatever you do over there, don't forget to bring back some gold," interrupted my mother.

"The people wear a lot of gold jewelry." I said." Don't you know your history? The Ashantis sit on gold. Even their chairs and swords are made of gold," said the mother.

"You might have been dating an African before. How did you know all that?" said my father in a jovial overtone. Mom pushed him aside.

"Are you jealous or joking? How dare you tell me that I am dating an African? I never saw any African in my school. They just weren't there by the time I was going to school. I only saw them in the movies."

"Mom, you might be joking. Africans are everywhere...."

"... not during my time in the forties ... even Negroes were invisible ... "

"I see ... that's why you do not know much about them.

"All that I know is what is shown in the movies." She then hesitated while pacing the floor.

I have to educate my people about the real Africans based on the little I know about Dora and her people. Now I realized the truth in Dora's statement that I would be the one to wipe away the ignorant bridge between the Africans and the Afro American. I stood up and stared at my mother.

"Mom, you mean you knew no African, not even while you were growing up?

"... I worked with this African lady, Debra, who used to boast all the time that she was a princess from Ashanti, whatever that means I don't know, She wore gold ornaments to work. I had to advise her to stop wearing expensive jewelry to work before she got robbed.

I took this opportunity to ask her a few questions about that Ashanti princess and she finally concluded that she hoped my friend would be from an Ashanti tribe. At least I have hooked them up and they had to agree with my intentions toward Dora. I could see from my mother's eyes that she seemed to admire her. Finally, before I left, both of them reluctantly told me that it was up to me to paddle my own lifeboat.

Having come that close with my parents, especially my mother, I had to deal with my sister also and come out with some consensus. I loved Darlene so much that I could not hide from her my long-range intentions about Dora.

"I think she would be a beautiful sister-in-law," I said to Darlene.

"What's going on? Who is getting married?" asked Darlene.

"You should understand what I mean about me getting married?"

"To whom...?" I hesitated to answer her because I needed no opposition from anybody.

"I am just in love...I think so," I said.

"With the African...?"

"Yes!"

"Well go for it. She is beautiful and would add beautiful children to our family if you plan to marry her," she gave her approval. I like her dimples when she smiles...," A sense of great joy filled my heart and I danced around like a pro.

On August 20, 1978, we attended a party organized by a friend of mine. I felt proud to take her to my people but before I knew it things had turned sour. The people started gossiping about her.

"Why do you encourage your brother to date an African?" said a friend to Darlene. I was close to them so I could hear their gossips but I pretended that I did not hear anything. My sister said nothing and stared at Dora constantly.

"If that's what she wants, the family will support him," answered Darlene.

"What about Yolanda...?" started the friend. At that point I joined them and changed the topic. Darlene advised me to go and be with Dora. It was like a fairy tale. Dora had vanished from the crowd. I became panicked and went outside looking everywhere for her. I thought someone had cornered her somewhere.

"Have you seen my woman?" I asked one of the guys."

"Your girlfriend; which one?" asked a fat man who smelled alcohol all around him.

"I am not joking," I said.

"You mean the African . . . ? She just left," he laughed. I became tensed and felt heavy. I could hardly move.

"Man, you are still worrying about that African? Don't you see all these beautiful chicks around here?" said the man. I ignored him and excused myself from the party. I went straight to her apartment on sixteenth but she was not home. I could not figure out where she had been. One thing I knew about her . . . she could spend the night with any of her people. My search for her that night proved no results. Two days later I found her but unfortunately her love for me was gone. With my kneels on the ground, I wanted to know what I did against her. She just moved away from me but I followed her quietly.

"I don't want to see you anymore," she said. "You are confused about me and my culture. I am an African I never wanted to be like anything else." I just had to let things cool down for a while. For almost two weeks we had not heard from each other. I was becoming Dora crazy and my family teased me that I was boo-whipped by the jungle girl whenever I visited them. I tried to get to her through her brother but I had no cooperation from him.

There was an elderly man, Mr. Mensa, among Dora's people, who had developed interest in me. He always used to tell me that I was a different Black-American. When I approached him about the problem I had with Dora, he offered to help me.

"You see, my son, Africans are cultured individuals and unless you understand the individual's culture and what you want to do with the person, you will hardly succeed to do anything with them," said Papa Mensah. He further advised me it wasn't easy to marry Dora because of where she came from in Africa where the parents control their daughter's marriages.

"What do I have to do?" I asked. He stressed that I had to know the culture and the norms of the people.

"Do you have some money before we start anything?" he asked.

"How much?"

"... at least $100.00," Papa Mensa said. I had no other choice than to bring out the money and to observe what the culture could contribute to bring Dora to my life. After handing the money to him, he asked me to follow him. We walked about six blocks and entered the home of an elderly lady.

"This is Nana Addae. She is the queen mother for Dora's people in this city. She can help you..." said Mr. Mensa. It was like I had just entered a classroom without knowing anything about the subject matter. I had never heard about a queen mother. All I knew is what my mother told me about the proud Ashanti lady who wore expensive jewelry. I kept my cool to wait on whatever they would do. After the introduction, two of them started speaking in heir language. This time their accent wasn't funny to me anymore. I wished I could speak and understand it.

"... a hundred dollars is not enough but we will manage it," said Nana Addae. I was curious to know what they would do.

"Perhaps we will give two pieces of cloth, two pairs of cloth and a jewelry." I heard two of them debating on these items.

"Okay, that will be fine. Since he doesn't know about the culture can you please do something for him," Mr. Mensa pleaded.

Nana Addae looked at me straight in the eyes and made me to understand that once I wanted to marry an African, I had no other choice than to do things in the African way.

"Even the white husbands, had to go by the dictates of the culture if they want an African wife," said Nana Addae.

"Whatever it will take to get my friend back I am willing to do"

"Now you are talking like a man," she said

"The whole thing will cost about $130.00 in order to be able to include gold a gold jewelry in what we plan to do," she said. I added the thirty dollars instantly. She advised us to come back the following day.

The next day, we joined Madam Addae to Dora's place. I imagined that she was surprised to see Papa Mensa and Madam Addae in her apartment. As for me she only stared at me and behaved as if I wasn't there. I really said to myself, "This is it." She greeted them in their language, and asked if they needed some water to drink. Nana Addae, who observed that she was ignoring my presence, rebuked her in their language and told her to welcome me too, according to their culture.

"Do you know this young man...?" There was a long period of silence.

"You are lucky I did not see you. I would not have opened the door." She addressed me indirectly.

"I hope this culture thing would work for me...," I murmured to myself.

"Stop that nonsense. What crime had he committed? Be considerate. He is a stranger to our culture; he is trying to be part of us through you," Nana Addae scolded Dora. It was like a cold water had been poured on her. She became speechless and politely asked me to have a seat in her yellow velvet sofa.

She brought us three glasses of water and then asked them why they were there with me. Nana Addae stood up and started speaking in their dialect. Mr. Mensa explained everything to me in English.

Dora we are here on behalf of Jason who says you are his friend from the school. To err is human and therefore he had offended you. That's part of the marriage game and therefore he had asked us to come and apologize on his behalf to forgive whatever he had done to offend you, he came with:

Two six yards of cloths, Two pairs leather shoes, a gold necklace, and two bottles of perfume. She became silent for a while before beginning to tell them the reason for her anger. Mr. Mensa silenced her without delay.

"You don't have to repeat anything. Nobody is a judge here. Just forgive and forget," Mr. Mensa said in a serious tone. With due respect to her elders, she accepted the gifts, hugged them and finally she hugged me. The cultural ingredient had worked for me this time. We became united again and she was happy for what I did for her.

From that experience, I became very courteous with her. I never played on her emotions again. I wasted no time to put wedding rings on lay away at the Montgomery Mall. Just as I was naive about her culture, so also she was naive about mine. I took her to the city Hall on July 18, 1978 and before she could know what was going on, we were at the justice of the peace. The court judge conducted the "I Do ' ceremony.

To me I became so elated for succeeding to call Dora my wife in my own terms. By August 3, 1978, we were living together in our new apartment. I frammed the marriage certificate and placed it in our bedroom. I read that certificate almost on daily basis but not once did I see Dora even looking at the certificate.

The first problem I encountered with Dora was about the phone. My friends called me very often on certain occasions, especially after the basket ball games, to chat about the outcome of the games and other things. We could not talk about the girls anymore. But I found out that she used the phone more than I did. Her people would be calling for her very constantly. All of these people would speak Twi and I became tired and bored to listen to her language even during dinner time. She had a habit of laughing and giggling on the phone while looking at me at the same time. Her attitude made me feel very uneasy at times but I kept my cool because I didn't want to offend her anymore.

Apart from the telephone ethic, there was no obvious problem between us until her people tried to dictate to us. Living with a woman for the first in a man's life is quite an experience. Perhaps our union worked so well because we were truly in love with each other and whenever she tried to be strange I knew how to caress her entire nervous system to get her sexually aroused at any moment. What I know is that I opened all doors of sexuality to her body that she was not thinking as an African anymore whenever we are in our sexual orientations. Our situation was far different from what my friends have been going through with their spouses.

When Emmanuel comes for visiting, I entertain him and promise to find him an American girlfriend. He would giggle when I converse about finding him a girlfriend.

"You are now my brother-in-law to be and make sure my sister orient you as what to do when you go to Ghana to see my parents," said Emmanuel.

"What do you mean by brother-in-law to be? I am your brother-in-law."

". . . I don't think so . . . unless you go to my country to ask my sister's hand from our parents."

"We are already married." My response prompted her and I tried to tell him that I wasn't joking. Dora heard her about our conversation from the bedroom.

"Emma and Jason what are you guys celebrating?" Dora asked. "What am I getting myself into," I murmured into myself. I pleaded to Emmanuel not to say anything to his sister about our little talk.

"We are fine. We are looking at the beautiful pictures in the Ebony Magazine. Emmanuel loves to see pictures of beautiful ladies," I replied. Later Dora asked me to follow her somewhere so we have to end our conversation."

The idea of going to my wife's country, have been bothering me for weeks. Many of her people who supported me have been asking me when I would go to see Dora's parents. It was a fine-looking African lady who revealed to me in confidence that, If I go to Ghana and Dora's parents concur to our marriage, it might set a precedence for others who are in love with Afro- American males but were afraid to get too involved because of the cultural bridges

I did not understand why the Africans had different perspective about relationships. I tried to ignore entertaining anything about going to cross the cultural bridges to Africa. As months passed my wife became very adamant about us going to Ghana for our final marriage rite. I contacted Madam Addae and Mr. Mensa for their advice. They told me the same story and once I have started the journey I have to finish it.

"Your mother-in-law is not an easy woman. African parents are totally opposite from your parents," concluded Mr. Mensa.

I came home lamenting about the whole scenarios about going to Africa. I could not just understand why I have to go to Africa to remarry my wife. I was kind of afraid of the wild animals I have been seeing on TV. "What about if I go there and I can't come back with Dora?" I murmured to myself. These thoughts were daunting on me. I felt something was touching me from behind. I turned around and there was Dora in a silky dress standing over my shoulders.

"Sweetheart, you may not understand but you can't proudly regard me as a wife unless we can have a final approval from my parents."

"At where?

"Ghana . . . ," she answered and then squeezed my shoulder and then looked straight into my eyes.

"There you go again. Whenever you go out to your people, you come home with all of this shit," I said. "You are a grown woman. Why can't you forget about that generation gap stuff.

"I did not know what I was getting myself into nor did you. How many of your people have married Africans. If you find any of them, you should learn from their experiences." Dora said to me calmly. "Do you know what is called culture?"

I could easily detect her mood swings so I kept mute to her questions. I decided to sit back and play it cool to make a sincere effort to learn more about her culture. I really needed someone from my culture who had married an African to learn of his experiences. I hardly could locate any American brother who has taken that route. I knew of few American sisters who have married African brothers they could not help me much since their marriage over here involved no cultural or parental barriers.

I kept looking across the country aiming to locate any African-American and African couple to learn something from them. I called everyone I knew but I got no positive results.

It was a big challenge because I realized that even though she loved me with her true heart but she very concerned about her parents. Whenever she came home she told a different story about my people or about the pressures her country people are giving her. One Wednesday she came home and gave me all the blues, blaming me for everything. I was just relaxing in my rocking chair when she walked in. I could feel the anger in her face as she slammed the door behind her.

"What's wrong, baby?" She never replied but I could tell by her vibes that she was disappointed about something. I stood in front of her expecting to get a kiss from her.

"Nothing is wrong with me but your people and their ways. They have no respect, whatsoever, for anything," she blamed. I had learned to be patient with her whenever she was in a bad mood but this time I felt within me like I was becoming a soft little punk. I was taking too much unnecessary shit from her. I stood up and spoke my mind.

"Let me tell you something . . . I am getting tired of your shifty little attitude and your damn mood swings," I proved my manhood.

"Oh! Now you want to show your real self. That kind of language . . . what kind of a teacher taught you that." Even though I knew she did not like me speaking slangs I was motivated to tell her how I felt in my own way.

"Let's be fair sometimes I don't like your African stuff, you're always blaming somebody for your mistakes," I yelled at her on a serious note. She felt guilty for something. It was then that she told me the truth that someone had taken her gold necklace at work and she was blaming me for nothing.

"Don't worry; I will replace that jewelry." she lifted her eyes and stared at me as if she had never seen me before.

"An incident like this compels people to visit voodoo houses . . . in Africa."

"Naw! Baby, don't do that. That voodoo shit scares me."

"Mind your language," she warned.

Within the preceding months my wife and I had become totally adjusted to each other. Both of us have come to understand each other's culture. For some time now she has not been complaining about anything in particular. What had been her song was that I would be a different husband after I have come back from Africa. "Who would like to go to Africa anyway?" I would murmur to myself.

Chapter Two

The decision of going to Africa had been bothering me. The last thing we needed was more drama to our relationship. I tried as much as possible to evade the topic. I suggested of seeking counsel about this idea of going to a strange place like Africa. My wife and I went to look for Mr. Mensa, but unfortunately we learnt that he had been deported. Dora's mood changed instantly.

"You see both the Blacks and the Whites are the same...," she retorted. Since I knew she was in a bad mood I did not respond to her comments but provided support to her outrage.

Perhaps I am thinking like my mother, who says funny things about Africa. Before I made my final decision whether to go to my wife's home or dissolve the marriage to avoid the journey I needed to know more about what the situation would be like in Africa. It was a difficult task to find an Afro-American like me, who had an African wife. I searched throughout the country to locate an African American like me who had similar experiences with an African lady. Luckily I was able to locate a schoolmate, Charles, who was stationed in Boston with his African wife. He actually discouraged me from going to Africa if possible. He had been to his wife's country so he gave me all the details about what to expect.

"Where in Africa did you go?" I asked.

"... Eastern Nigeria," he said."

"Well, my wife is different. She is from Ghana," I concluded.

"My brother, it makes no difference which part of Africa, the whole continent is nothing but a sea of customs and tribal divides. It's entirely different from ours," said Charles. "You know another name for Africa should be Cultural Enclave.

"My wife is an Ashanti and I have read quite a bit about the Ashantis. Just tell me what I need to take with me."

"Ashanti! That's even worse . . . the people who sit on gold. You need to take with you every culture you -down to earth type of a thing, respect to elders and pray hard. I can assure you today that you do not have a wife yet," said Charles.

I got pissed off when he said that shit to me. All the shit that I've gone through to win her love would be in vain?

"Don't go to Africa with that mentality of the government. The governments over there have nothing to do with the people's social system. The family does everything." Charles further convinced me.

"So what do you suggest I do?"

"You need luck and lots of money in addition to your own personality and culture."

"What a fuck are you talking about-where is culture in America? Excuse my expression," I said.

"I am used to this type of expression as we all did when we were younger." said Charles. "Africa is a big continent . . . many cultures and unique social fabrics."

"I know what I am talking about because I have been there. The people consider our court marriage as the white man's thing."

"How much money would I need?" I asked. "It all depends on your wife's family. In my case I stayed in a hotel because my in-laws had refused to honor the relationship at the first sight"

I did not like the idea of going to my wife's country to face all of the drama mentioned by Charles. As an African in a Diaspora, I never dreamed that black lovers would have to go through such a challenge. Since then, I had been asking Dora to tell me what would be expected of me. She gave me simple answers.

"It all depends," she would say. "I don't even know much about the culture; all that I know is that you need to take some dowry to my people and the elders will give us their blessings." I would never get anything concrete from my wife. She was only occupied with shopping for the things to take along with us during our journey. She bought many things . . . from needles to the golden ornaments. Within six weeks, five suitcases were full; each weighed more than seventy pounds.

"How many suit cases are we taking along with us. We will be embarrassed at the airport with all these with us.

"Wait until you get to the airport. There you will know what it means to travel to African."

"This was the bridge and ignorance I was talking about. Though we are different from your friend wife's people yet Africans are the same wherever they may be," she said. "So what actually do you expect me to do...?" I asked.

We have been together for about a year now; my whole family had got used to her. Sometimes my little brothers and cousins would make fun of her accent but not in her presence. She often visited with gifts for the children. They loved her for that. One Friday afternoon, we passed by my parent's place. Daddy was very excited to see us and cracked a joke. He told us how he dropped out from school at age sixteen to join the army. But we kept laughing at him. For some reason Dora decided to address her concerns.

"I am ready for you all to see my father," My father looked at her and seemed confused about her request. "You mean to go to Africa...?" asked my father. My mother came from the kitchen and intervened. Dora knew that my parents were as ignorant as I was about them and ceased asking any further questions. My father called me outside and wanted to know what she meant but I was as uninformed as he was. "Africans live in their own world and whatever it is I will explore it," I said and tapped my father on the shoulders. I made a joke we all laughed.

I wish you good luck," he said. Even when I was deployed I never wanted to go to Africa but for some reason, the white soldiers loved to go there," said my father

"Didn't that prove something?"

"Their cousin Tarzan is white," he joked and we all laughed,We left my parent's place with both of us having mixed feelings. She wanted to know if I was offended when she talked to my father. I had to do a lot of explanation. Both of us realized that we had cultural bridges that are defined differently to cross. At least she is more exposed to my cultural ingredients than I am to hers. So this question of visiting Africa continues to daunt me.

Five days later, Charles returned my call.

"You would have to convince the family that you are a responsible husband and can take care of their daughter. If the father rejects you must forget the marriage. If they reject, especially the Father or the one who helped with her education, you must as well forget. No government can save your black ass over there," he said to me while laughing over the telephone.

"Did you go with your marriage certificate?" I asked.

"You need to forget that marriage certificate shit. The cultural bridge you are crossing know no governments but rather parents. Over there girls are hot cakes to the parents because they are sources of expensive dowries, if you know what I mean." I could not convince myself that the cultures would be exactly the same.

"You have been a great help to me and hope, no matter how difficult it would be to cross the bridge, I pray that I would be successful," I convinced myself.

The government itself operates like a foreigner on a foreign land. To me the better governance for the people is their cultural institution. The people's culture is much more powerful than any institution. I am telling you what I know, you better believe and respect their way of life, while you are with them. You only need the government when you want to do anything associated with the white folks or the western world's culture.

"Anyway tell me exactly what happened." I wish I had not asked. I could not believe when he told me that his in-laws would not accept his dowry due to the fact that the wife was their first-born. According to her culture, the first child is never allowed to marry anyone outside their tribal enclave."

"He had to be a man from the village and the parents did not want to set any bad precedence. I almost shit on myself when he told me that.

"My wife is an Ashanti and Ashantis might be different from the Ibos," I said.

"Have you been listening to anything I've been telling you all these weeks? I don't give a damn if your wife is Ashanti, Kalami or Salami, it doesn't matter; don't try to compare your wife's country and my wife's country; their culture is all the same. I will be glad when you finally take your black ass over there and see for your damn self."

"Don't expect me to know, comprehend and accept this overnight what you know already about your experiences with these people; "I am not pushing you into anything but I'm advising you to keep you away from disgrace and disappointment when you go over there," said Charles with a soft tone. "This is the time to prove to the family that you would be a responsible husband and can take care of their daughter at all cost."

"This is crazy! My goodness. Did she tell her parents that you're rich or something?"

"She doesn't have to. I keep telling you-this is a cultural thing."

"So how much are we talking about now . . . ?" I asked.

"In my case I spent $3,000 in addition to all the gifts we took with us . . .

"Man! Don't play with me." Charles kept silence for a while. I realized I was being difficult for him.

"Jason!" he called my name loud

"I am here. I haven't gone anywhere . . . "

"Do you know what time is it?"

"I looked at the clock on the wall. We had talked for about forty-five minutes.

"I know you're fed up with me . . . "

Oh no! I just want to help you out. In my case I was able to maneuver through their cultural barrier. I had no other choice because I loved Nancy Oby, I call her my African Queen. I won't lie to you. I borrowed some money."

"What made them change their mind?" I asked with the intention to collect as much information as I could.

"My luck was our sweet eighteen month old daughter, Onicha. God so good I gave her an African name over the rejection of my parents-who was with us, else my wife would not have come back with me." My daughter was a factor for our marriage.

"Dora and I don't have a baby yet

"That would have helped you but it doesn't matter now. Just go and demonstrate to them that you love their daughter. I know whatever African thing they come out with, God would provide a way."

"Oh! Yes! You have said the magic word. May God bless it."

"I wasn't a total stranger. My in-laws had already got plenty of information on me. They knew I treat Nancy like a queen. What you need to do is to stop bitching and crying like a little baby. Just do what you gotta do man.

Sometimes I wondered why I should go through such a lynching experience. I have learnt a lot to respect human beings and their cultures, knowing that there are more to human existence than what we have been taught to know. If I had to go through the father and the mother, brothers and sisters to earn a relationship, then of course, I would have to respect this institution. Charles advised me to carry along dozens of handkerchiefs, perfume and cologne, watches and whatever else I could get. Since Dora was doing the extravagant shopping as if we were children of some rich tycoons, I did not have to do anything concerning the shopping. I could also agree with her because Dora is a hard-working lady. Sometimes I wondered how she got her energy to work round the clock. Even my sister Darlene commented on her attitude about life.

One day while I was out of town, Dora took Darlene to one of their African functions. Since that day she has been telling everyone in my family that I had married a very prominent African lady. But until now, she never told anybody what she saw about Dora at the African function.

"She is just too complicated . . . she is just too much . . . and the beauty and brains she has it all," said my sister, when I was trying to make her tell me what she knew about Dora. I was very happy for Darlene to accept my wife in principle. I wondered where she learnt all these about my wife.

"She is no different from any other woman."

"Brother, you don't know what you have. She is not one of these wild gun smoking, hootchie mamas. She is a bad sister. . . first class all the way."

Usually Darlene never talked like that and I wondered if she was drunk or something.

"I thank you for your observation and praises. Make sure you tell mom and dad this." All arrangements were ready for the journey. I have just obtained my visa from the Embassy and I was surprised I didn't have to go through any scrutiny or strict security clearance. Dora obtained all the necessary papers on my behalf. Within three days my visa was ready. I was kind of reserved to inform my parents that I was going to Africa. Finally, three days before our departure, I informed my parents and asked for some contribution toward my expenses. I was only trying my luck; perhaps, I should not have asked.

"Son, you have all my blessings. You are of age and if this is what you want to do, the best I could do is to wish you good luck." That's not what I really wanted to hear from daddy. According to Charles, I might run out of money while I am in Africa but my father is kind of hard on money. We had to work hard before we could get any money from him even though he is very lenient in giving on special holidays or occasions.

"Daddy, I have been advised that I have to go to Africa to marry my wife again from her parents." I became as sober as I could and waited for his remark.

"That was what she was trying to tell you last time when she was here. Both of us never understood her either."

"What about me?" Is she going to marry you from me . . . ?"

Daddy . . . it's their culture and there is nothing we can do . . . unless I change my mind on her."

"You put me in this. I know what you can do . . . take your married certificate over there and show it to them."

I could not convince my father to render any financial help, Mom heard our conversation from the kitchen. She would have been the last person I would tell. She is still not too convinced about my decision. She just wasn't sure what I would get out of Africa. She came and intervened in our discussion.

"Didn't you watch in the movies yesterday? Tarzan was watching over an African tribal marriage ceremony. The people behaved and dressed like the cave men with that white man sitting among them as their king."

"My wife is not from that part of Africa; she is an Ashanti." I moved closer to both of them and showed them some pictures and scenes from Ghana.

"Son, we're not against your wishes. I am behind you all the way but make sure you bring your ass back home. I could not withstand all the sarcastic remarks from my parents. I left their presence to deal with my friend

Chapter Three

During our journey to the motherland, we stopped over in London. Dora met many people from Ghana that she knew. I looked everywhere but I never saw a single person I knew. That taught me a big lesson; the world is much broader, beyond my expectations. She introduced me to none of her people but I never fussed about it. Since it was my first flight abroad, I was curious observing everything.

"Thanks for this journey, I feel so good now. How come you know many people over here?" I asked Dora.

"This is London . . . our home; I mean our colonial base?"

"That's wonderful to see your people in such high spirits; I am already excited."

"Wait until we arrive home then you can arrive at your conclusions." At this time it was announced that we should board our flight to Accra. Fifteen minutes later, all of us were seated and the plane taxied off from the ground. When the plane took off into the British airspace, it was like I was in Africa. The passengers gaily spoke African languages. Few of them spoke English or mixed their sentences with the African language and the English. I could detect that they were very happy to go home. Seeing Africans in such great numbers, for the first time, many strange thoughts entered me and I wondered how I had been brainwashed, throughout my school days, about other people. I experienced my first cultural shock when we landed in Accra on March 28, 1980 12 noon. I stood at the airport and pondered over how foolish I had been for imagining that I was going to a jungle place. Walking from the Pan Am Airline to the main terminal I could not convince myself that I was in Africa until I saw the airport sign 'AKWAABA-WELCOME

TO KOTOKA INTERNATIONAL AIRPORT', ACCRA-GHANA. Everywhere around me was crowded with people of my kind- managing all the affairs in their own way and capacity and of course in their own country. The checking in was a bit rough but my wife, understanding their system of bribery we passed through the customs with ease.

When Darlene told me that my wife is great like a queen I could not believe her. Today I saw many signs of it at the airport. I could not understand that many relatives of Dora came all the way from the village to welcome her. Her people were excited to see her as if she had been lost for decades. I could see their excitement from a distance. They clapped, and called her name. There were more than fifteen people at the airport to welcome Dora. A young guy got my luggage from me and said, "thank you."

"What is he thanking me for?" I muttered. They shook hands with Dora, hugged each other and laughed among themselves. I waited for a long time for Dora to introduce me to her people but nothing like that happened. I contemplated that she might have talked about me in their dialect following the dictates of their culture.

When we came outside to taxis and vehicles stand, there was a twenty-two seat Mercedes van waiting outside for Dora. I was enjoying the tropical heat and the cool ocean breeze. Our luggage and other traveling accessories were packed at the top of the Benz. We all found ourselves seated in the van. The people were staring at me when I boarded the van, both Dora and I occupying the front seats. "Are you not going to introduce me? I whispered in her ears. She just rolled her palm on my thigh. Before the driver took off, he asked Dora in English, "where is your friend's destination?" Dora did not respond? "...to the embassy?" continued the driver. Still Dora hesitated to answer him.

"I don't know what you mean, but this is my wife?" I held Dora's hand.

"Your wife?" A young lady questioned from the back seat. Thoughts of Charles, who advised me about some experiences I might encounter with my wife's family, popped out in my mind.

No! Not with me," I murmured to myself. It seemed that there was much confusion, giggling, laughing, and expecting more explanation from Dora. She kept quiet and never said a word.

"Don't worry. None of these people is my father or mother. Just be nice to everybody. You are with me," Dora said softly in my ears. The conversation between them lasted for a while. I held my peace and began to enjoy the scenes in the city while they were mumbling in their language. Fifteen minutes later, the driver stopped in front of a beautiful building. "We have to get down," said Dora. I became confused. Both of us stared at each other. The driver's mate was on top of the van taking out some of our luggage with Dora's instructions.

"You are going to dump me to leave me stranded?"

Before I knew what was going on, the van moved away with all our stuff. Luckily, Dora was left with me. This was the time I wished I was back in the States especially when Dora waved at them. The memories of Charles and all his crazy ass talks revisited me.

Fortunately, the place was a small classic hotel, lodged by mostly foreigners because the bills could be paid with foreign currency.

The lobby was occupied with other foreigners from different countries. In fact, the African accent, that we used to laugh at in the States, was far better than some of the accents that were spoken at the hotel lobby. Dora took the time and patience after we had relaxed, to explain certain things to me.

"I was advised to stay here with you to acquaint you more with the culture."

"What culture again?"

"I can't just go to my parents with you to introduce you to them that you are my husband. You see, whatever your friend told you is right," Dora broke the ice.

"Anyway let's put the cultural thing behind I need to see the city"

You are in a different world, a different social fabric and a world of intense culture," explained my wife.

"I don't want to hear about your people again until tomorrow after I have visited our embassy."

I was just jiving. The cultural stuff was still entangling us in the hotel. They left Dora's little sister behind. This girl was watching everything we did.

Charles advised me to try to develop fervent love for my wife's people, especially toward her brothers and sisters. Those individuals, if they love you could convince their hard rock parents on my behalf. They can be part of the decision making process before a marriage could be determined. Stella and I quickly became friends.

"Do you want to go to America?" I asked. She looked at me hard and giggled showing a feeling of shyness.

"Yes," she nodded in agreement.

"Okay. I will take you to America with me." She lifted up her head and gave me a wide smile from her face. "Help me so that your sister becomes my wife." I must admit, I felt kind of cheap literally, bribing this little girl just to solidify my relationship with my own damn wife. Before she could say anything Dora came out from the bathroom and interrupted our brief conversation. She said something to her in their language and Stella became very quiet.

"I hope she understood whatever you were saying to her," said my wife. I did not say anything and I could read from Stella's countenance that she was elated about my offer.

An hour later, Dora hired a taxi to drive us through the city for sightseeing. It was a beautiful sightseeing experience. The driver took us to many important places in the city, starting from the university, airport area, the ministries, the beach, market areas and an illuminated roundabout known as "Kwame Nkrumah Circle and many other places. This was a heck of an experience for me. Later the driver dropped us at a club and promised to pick us up within two hours.

The socialization at the club was far different from clubs back home. Everybody was relating to each other as if they were all brothers and sisters. There was no fuss over whi is dancing or chatting with who. They sang together, hugged each other and shared drinks and snacks among themselves. That was something beyond my comprehension. That was the moment I wished I was not married, I would have picked any one of the beautiful sisters in the club. When I went to the bartender to order some drinks, they knew instantly that I was an Afro-American. As if someone had passed the word around; three white guys came to our table. "Hey what's up?" said one of the white guys.

"Nothing much, just enjoying my first visit."

"I see that; you want to marry one of them already; she pointed to Dora. You chose the most beautiful one. Congratulations," said one of them. My wife tapped my foot with hers and glowed with a mile. Before the White guy and I could continue our conversation, a slim young African brother came over to our table. "Hey Akosua, when did you come back...?" Asked the guy. He then asked to dance with her without asking permission from me. My wife politely said that she would be back. I sat there shaking my head. This is the time the white guys got the opportunity to get closer to me.

"I know how you feel. Let's forget the differences we have at home. Here we know ourselves as unique Americans, that color stuff is out of the vocabulary over here," said one of the guys.

"I know, its fucked up back home. We have all the racial bullshit and when we travel abroad, we Americans, regardless of our color we stick together," I said.

"What we have here is the culture . . . which we lack at home. These people are different and the best part of it is that they are humanly harmless." He could see that I was worried about the guy dancing with my woman.

"I see . . . ," I said

"Do you think . . . in our culture someone can grab your woman to dance without asking permission from you? This is just a typical African behavior." I held unto his hands and squeezed them. I can't explain what made me do that. . . .

"Thanks for your advice. I know it will help me a lot," I said.

"It makes no sense to fight over a woman over here," said the other. Even though I related to what they were saying, I couldn't help myself from keeping my eyes from Dora who was still dancing in the middle of the dancing-floor. . I was a little jealous but I played it cool.

"Have you met her people yet?" asked Jim, one of the white guys

"No we just arrived.

"This is not America; over here it is the justice of the parents rather than the justice of the peace. That's my advice to you and I hope you understand. Jim took a bottle of beer and poured some into the glass. He drank it very fast and encouraged me to drink something. I was kind of confused about what he said but I felt reserved to ask for any explanations.

"Jim, you seem to have more experience about this people . . . ," I tried to say something.

"You just have to know and understand their ways. They are entirely different people from what we know about them from home," he said and then ordered for more drinks.

"If your wife happened to come from the Ashanti tribe, then you will face two tough scenarios: justice of the parents and justice of the Ashanti culture. I hope she is not from a royal family." Instantly, I took a deep breath, trying not to recapture any more fears within me.

"You make it seem like I'm an amateur mountain climber who can fall off from the cliff at anytime." Jim just stared at me without commenting on my remark. For some reason he asked me to take my wife away from the place before she ran into an old school mate or boyfriend. Dora has now finished dancing and seated herself beside me.

"My name is Jim from Albany, New York, I am a Peace Corps Volunteer," Jim introduced himself.

"Nice meeting you. My name is Akosua Dora; we just arrived from the States." Just as soon as we came out, my hope was to see the taxi driver, a young, white guy approached us from the opposite end of the street.

"If you guys want to have some real fun, let me take you to "O Jay's Corner. It's not far from here," he said. I stood there motionless for a while pondering over the down to earth behavior of the white guys over here.

"You'll see before you leave this place, wonders will happen... you have not seen anything yet," Dora whispered in my ears. Soon after that a wooden truck, with an inscription "TRAVEL AND SEE," written on both sides of the vehicle, came by. The sign told many stories affecting my experiences in Africa. It opened my eyes to many things.

"I know what you are thinking about, but in Africa that color stuff does not exist. The people are too nice to be discriminated against," he said.

"I can see that... you don't even know us."

"You don't have to know anybody to hook up with the person. Your wife will tell you that," he said. "Any way my name is Kwame." They shook their hands. While I pondered over what kind of name was Kwame, especially for a white guy, Dora laughed. She perceived my thoughts. I felt like I was being sandwiched.

"My name is Jason and this is my wife... Dora." Dora shook his hand.

"It's nice to meet you all. I am due to get married myself to an African but her mother seem to be a stumbling block." I just did not want to hear anything of this again so I changed the topic. We agreed to go and visit the 'Oh Jay's Corner' for brief moment.

We found ourselves totally underdressed over there. I saw a few brothers and sisters getting their grooves on. I became so excited at this place and I wished I had gone there alone. We sat at a dark corner with Kwame. I could not move my eyes away from the only hostess in the place, a slim fat booty sister, I am assuming she is a local. My wife knows I am a ladies watcher so she was always watching me when we go out. Whenever the hostess came around, she would be looking at my face. I wished I could dance with her. Kwame realized that my mind was far away without taking note of the drinks he had just ordered for us. He encouraged us to drink and then go to the floor to dance. To his disappointment, we chose not to dance at that time. But that gave him an opportunity to put his nose into our business. He then wanted to know how I met my wife.

"I hope she is not from the Twi tribe?" said Kwame. Twi was a new word to me.

"What's that...Twi?" I asked.

"You haven't taught him anything about your people?" he asked my wife.

"Not much...that's the reason why I brought him here. Africa to them is all jungle land." "I know what you mean. I'm white and I thought the same way until I joined the Peace Corps. My experiences in this country, especially with the Ashantis have opened my eyes." I will never be the same again. The people are just smart, wise and pompous. "How does this help me?" I murmured to myself.

"I am an Ashanti. My parents live in Kumasi," said Dora. "I just want him to see the capital city first before we travel to Kumasi."

We came back to the hotel. Maybe, it was the whole thing of being in Africa, you know, the whole Mandingo thing. All I could think about was getting in between the sheets with Dora. That was all that was in my mind. Even God will blame me for that if I fail to have my first sex in Africa with my wife during the first day. I don't think any culture will prevent that. When Dora and I got into our sheets and wanted to do my thing she simply refused. I struggled quietly but she won't let me. Now I came to conclusion that Dora sent me to Africa to disgrace or dump me. I was really furious and had wanted to drive her away from the room. I might have got a chance with that beautiful slim receptionist who was eyeing me when I first entered the lobby. She saw the extent of my fury. She moved over and held me tight with a kiss.

"Don't you know my sister is in the next room?" She said to me. My eyes became reddish at once. I sat on the pillow and bounced myself.

"What a hell does that mean . . . part of the tribal stuff?" I screamed. The noise awakened her for a brief moment but she quickly went back to sleep, disturbing nothing.

"We can't do that now. . . my sister is here." She was just jiving with an excuse.

"The girl is sound asleep. She cannot hear us." I had to beg this time. "Else we can go to the bathroom. . . ." I suggested patiently. For some reason nothing I said changed her mind. She cannot have sex while her sister was around. I was so disappointed that we stayed awake most of the night.

"Are you interested in me as a wife or as your sex machine? You need to pray for God to open a way instead of you always contaminating your chances."

I have a diary of the first things that happened in my life. The first time I dated, ever kissed a woman, cursed, fought on the street, fought in school, suspended from school, made love to a woman, and the list goes on and on. I wanted to add to my list of memories, the sexiest things I did when I went to Africa. How would that sound if I listed that I admired a beautiful hostess at a bar? I felt asleep with these thoughts on my mind.

Ironically, after we have played our usual romance and got me on the mood. She came out with some cultural excuses.

She told me that their culture demands that I have to complete going through the marriage rituals before we can have sex once we are in her country.

"That's crazy. I don't want to hear this rite stuff again. What do you mean by that?" You are sitting here stroking. . .I'm as hard as rock and you blame me. . . . ?

"I mean it. This is Africa. I think you need to go and look for the white guys we met in town. He was trying to tell you something at the bar but your eyes were all over the hostess serving at the bar." I sat up in the bed . . . visualizing the wooden truck with the inscription 'TRAVEL AND SEE.' I comforted myself with those words and before I knew it I felt asleep in a lonely bed while she went and slept with her sister. I can't believe this shit. All the advice Charles explained to me, I have experienced the worst today.

On Saturday, our relationship was tensed. She knew what I could become when she refuse me sex. But now that I am in her home she is taking this advantage of me. I could not do much this Saturday, my mind was everything else besides her. She felt it so toward the evening she suggested that we should go to the movies in the evening. That excited me for I never knew that they had movie theatres. I prayed that Stella would not go with us since it might be an X-rated movie. When I asked her where Stella would be she became hyper.

"She is going with us . . . there are no rated, Ex-rated or what have you movies in this country. You are still dreaming about America but you will forget it very soon." I could not argue. Before long Stella excited about what her sister had told her about us going to the movies.

About 6:30 P.M we found ourselves sitting in a medium sized theater called "Orion" and curiously waited for the screen to open. When the movie started, the audience began whistling across the hall. The screen brightened with colored lights and the title "Tarzan Jungles" was showing on the screen. There was a prolonged roar "Tarzan! Tarzan! . . . echoed throughout the cinema hall.

"What's the fuck, is this . . . showing this damn movie over here?" I said to my wife.

"What's wrong about it? This is the type of movie the people love to watch in addition to Indian and the America Cowboy movies. The irony was very difficult for me to grasp, after seeing the negative stereotypes of Tarzan on our TV screens since my infancy. The African characters in the Tarzan movies had been given a nickname by the Africans, portraying people who had no origin on the African Continent.

"Don't you all see how demeaning this Tarzan shit is? This is embarrassing to your people," I said.

"Who cares? That's what they did to keep you away from Africa. Now you are here so you won't be thinking like them anymore." I thanked her so much for taking me to the movies before going to her village because that changed my perception about Africans greatly. It was Stella and I who watched the pictures to the end; Dora slept comfortably on my lap. We returned from the movies about 10:00 pm. This night Dora could not hold on to her cultural restrictions. She became so cozy that she cleared a way for us to have a sneaky sex. She sent Stella to give a note to the desk clerk. Only

God knows what the note was about. As soon as Stella left she undressed herself and I followed right away. I thought we had to sneak to do this but my expectation was wrong.

"Nobody should know we are doing this," she warned. I did not play with her at all, I made her feel that she was a woman and only the right man can bring a woman out of a woman. Within two hours I had the strength to enter into her in a way that she will never forget me-culture or no culture. She became exhausted and laid flat as soft as the cotton wool.

"Why did you think I brought you to Africa to face this fight. You bring my womanhood out of me and I don't think I will ever get another man like you." I relaxed her by caressing her. She picked up the phone and spoke in her language. She told me to pretend to be sleeping. Five minutes later Stella came in with some fried fish and bread. They ate some and then slept together. I felt like the king of the jungles, going over this cultural bridge.

On Sunday we stayed inside for most of the day. Many people came to our hotel to look for Dora. I slept most of the day while she was associating with her people. I had no reason to be jealous of anything because the people relate differently with each other. Some were happy to see me around Dora and others registered their disapproval by frowning. I was extraordinary nice to those who tried to chat with me. Getting to the evening two ladies arrived. Dora welcomed them warmly. Stella also stood up and hugged them. I became curious of whom they might be. I wished that they did not have to stay with us overnight. We needed our privacy. After an hour Dora saw them off. Even though they seemed to be educated but they never spoke a word of English. Later I learnt that they were family members who came on behalf of the family to enquire when Dora would be going to the village.

"The early we go the better," Dora commented.

On Monday I was the first person to enter through the gate of the American Embassy to register my presence in that country. That was what I was advised to do by the Peace Corp guys. The receptionist was a Ghanaian lady who knew Dora. Having known my mission she asked me if I was really serious to marry an Ashanti woman like Dora? I nodded affirmatively. She didn't say anything again.

"Is he going to your area?" said a slim white lady who was standing behind the receptionist.

"Yes," Dora answered.

"Why are they being nosy. Is this their business . . . ,? I mumbled.

"Good luck," she said and then she left the scene. Soon after that, Dora and the lady began to speak their language. Stella just giggled while they were talking. Instantly I became panicked.

"What's going on?" I questioned my self. I knew they had to be talking about me. I just hoped it was something good. She then began to speak English with an offer.

"I will do my best to make sure you marry this girl and take her back to America," said the receptionist. "Any way my name is Mary Nkrumah," she introduced herself.

"Nice to meet you; my name is Jason Washington." We shook each other.

"That's a nice name." She tapped me on the shoulder and promised that she would do whatever she could to help me.

Chapter Four

During the early morning hours on Tuesday we had to pack up our things for the next journey. There wasn't much I could do since the master plan was with Dora. She told me to be calm for God was already on my side. By eight o'clock in the morning, we were in line at the lobby to check out. I could not keep my eyes away from the desk clerk who make Black people proud with her mind-boggling dark complexion. "Black is beautiful indeed," I murmured to myself. Then I debated within me what brought the phrase black is beautiful in the first place? Even though I have been here just for a few days but I am convinced and proud of being black. Even though I had a crush on her but she never noticed it. She and my wife were engaged in a conversation and giggling at each other. She never stole a look at me. The checking out wasn't that smooth. They seemed to be holding us when the manager came from behind and they started talking in their dialect. I wish I knew what was the problem. In the end they shook hands and bid us farewell.

We left the hotel into the crowded streets where we hired a taxi to the bus terminal. Dora had already explained to me that she wanted me to experience every aspect of their culture so we would be mingling with the people and I should not let that bother me. We had enough money to chatter a taxi to our destination but we decided to take this mode of transportation. I was impressed to see big buses like the Greyhound buses in the States. They call them government transport, air conditioned with cushioned seats.

"You people live a life like Americans but why don't you talk when people are laughing at you?" I asked my wife. She stared at me and then raised her head unto the skies and shook her head. I really don't understand what that meant.

"You have not seen anything, keep all your questions until later. You may find the answers by yourself," she replied calmly. She bought a few things from the station vendors. Dora was right Africa was like a different world. They do everything differently. Vendors would be talking loud to customers to persuade them to buy their goods. To my dismay other vendors would actually go inside the bus to sell to the customers. There was one preacher vendor who spent about ten minutes preaching to the passengers. The passengers in the end, turned to be his congregation and they gave him their tithe.

This is the time I I felt the urge to understand the language. Luckily Dora had told Stella to speak to me only in their dialect. She had her own trick to teach me the language with the aid of the hand. She would touch my hand and then say it in their dialect. {hand=nsa; head=etire; mouth=ano; I=me; house=efie; sleep=da; take=fa; food=aduane; take the food= fa aduane no. etc etc} Before I knew it, I was getting some understanding of the language. There was nothing funny about it any more. The bus took off at about 10:00 o'clock in the morning. My eyes were filled with nothing but curiosity. What would I expect to see on the road for this journey of over two hundred miles into the hinterland. Soon after that I became an adventurer in the world of the unknown. What I knew of Africa is not what I am seeing today

About twenty miles on the road, I had already burdened my eyes to satisfy my curiosity. It was like I was passing through a farmers market with fresh produce, life chicken and wild meat. I live in the city and the sources of the items in the supermarkets are unknown to me. The roads we were traveling on was a two-way narrow road that passes through villages, towns and farms. Dora kept looking at me as my eyes were always looking out in the window on the side and straight ahead of me, depending on the view.

Along the road were farms with grooves of orange trees, mangoes, bananas families, some small some big and among these big fruit trees grew tomatoes, okra, pepper, greens and many other edible plants that I have never seen before. In between these farms were small villages where the farmers lived. One thing I never saw was farming machines nor trucks. The first big town we came to was city at the bottom of some mountain ranges The driver had a fifteen minute stop and we all got down to stretch our legs. It was like a commercial center and everyone here was a vendor. Tens of vendors came around the vehicles that had stopped. There were nice concrete buildings, some two and three storey buildings. "Where is this place?" I asked my wife. "You guys are happy over here."

"What did I tell you? Keep all your curiosity to yourself and the answers will come later," she reiterated. It was Stella who hinted me that the people come down from the mountains to trade. She pointed to the right and I could that the north east part was lined up with a long scarp raised up about a mile below sea level.

"How do people go up there?" I asked Dora.

"Cars go up there but to me I won't go there," she said.

My curiousity ended when we boarded the board I observed that in every village or town we passed, the trees that provided shades against the sun rays bore edible fruits. Those that I could identify were orange trees, pears, mango trees, coconut trees etc. I was also on an expedition to watch wild life. What interested me most was the species of the birds that I saw, both big and small. These birds have multiplicity of colors. The beautiful colored birds appealed to my eye and I wished I could photograph them "These are the type of things we need to see in our books," I murmured to myself.

Dora opted to explain certain things to me to ease my curiosity. When I spoke the passengers realized I was an Afro-American. There was a gentleman in the middle seat and having heard my accent he stretched his hand and handed over to me a small pamphlet. I thanked him and then gave it to my wife. She looked at the title "Oh we thank you very much Sir," said my wife.

"You need to study this before we arrive . . . it's very important that you know this." The way was now opened for the rest of the passengers to talk to her. They asked her questions about me but all was dictated in her language.

I concentrated my attention on the little booklet. I never put it down until I read it more than four times.

WELCOME TO THE GARDEN CITY

Kumasi, the capital of Ashanti is situated in the center Ghana, about two hundred and seventy miles from the capital. It is a historical city. The early white men, who had no idea that The souls of Ashantis were united together as one body attempted to fight them in order to control their minerals rich land. While in

Kumsai, learn more about the Ashanti wars against the British Visit the cultural center and the Kumasi Fort to acquaint yourself with the people's past. There is much to be said about the people and their history. I can only give some brief highlights and allow you, the reader, to make a thorough research about Ashantis while you are with them. In Kumasi, the first thing that should come to mind is the Manhyia Palace, the King's official office and residence. It is the center of the whole Ashanti Nation and permanent museum of war artifacts and the cultural arts and crafts.

Kumasi without Okomfo Anokye is like a king without a stool. Okomfo Anokye was a divine soul who purposely came to make the Ashanti nation powerful and unconquerable from their enemies. While in Ashanti, bear in mind that the institution of chieftaincy is very strong.

You may hear names like Nana Yaa Asantewaa, Nana Osei Tutu and Okomfo Anokye. Those were great ancestors of the region. Pay respect to those names and others.

Ashantis have little western influence in the way they do things because the white man could not interfere in their way of life as they did to the other African tribes. They love to speak their language, Twi, so don't hesitate to learn it.

What is impossible in the western world can always be possible in Africa and Ghana in particular. While in Kumasi, don't try to do anything stupid against the norm of the society. The citizens can take the law into their own hands and offenders could be beaten to death.

Don't expect to see police officers driving around. You are in a third world country. Depending on your length of stay, you may not see a police officer apart from those directing traffic at some go slow junctions, unless you go to the police station where they comfortably sit and relax themselves, waiting for citizens to come to them for complaints.

THE CITY'S NICKNAME IS 'THE GARDEN CITY OF WEST AFRICA.

Have a nice stay

After reading the booklet, lots of thoughts plumaged through my mind.

"Thank you very much. Do you want it back?" I asked the man who gave me the booklet.

"No! It's yours. You will need that thing all your life. My brother lives somewhere in overseas country and he advised me to write something like this to aid people such as yourself

"Thank you...this has acquainted me with many things I did not know."

Finally as the driver sped along, the scenes on the side of the roads changed. The villages and the towns began to conglomerate together, the people appear to be diverse in terms of what they were wearing, manner of trade and traffic flow increased in all directions. The homes were built with concrete blocks and roofed with iron sheets. It seemed that the people had no fear of the moving vehicles. They crossed the streets any how without minding the traffic. To satisfy my anxiety, I spotted a big signboard: Kwame Nkrumah University of Science and Technology.

"Where are we . . . scenes are drastically changing," I asked Dora.

"I am glad you are observant . . .we are in the Garden City-Kumasi our destination."

"So you have a University here?"

"What do you think of this place? You are now in the Garden City of West Africa, you are not at home any more." Before I could satisfy my curiosity, the scene had passed.

As we went closer to the inner city I learnt that I was in a humane world. The houses were so close to each other that there was no room for any neighbor to have hated each other. There would have no room for the neighborhood children to have hate and fight each other. "Is this the reason why these people relate to each other like a big family in my country?" I grumbled. People-children, adults, vendors, pedestrians were everywhere. Dora was pointing to some Landmarks but I had no meaning to them at that time. I was so elated to be here. A van, with an inscription "HOME SWEET HOME," passed by. Soon I noticed that all the no commercial vehicles have a phrase from the owner to the public inscribed on their sides, back or front.

The last destination was on a hill overlooking a valley. We got our luggage together and Dora asked Stella to watch over them. "Are your people coming to get us?" I asked because I wanted to put up a different show.

"No, nobody knows we are here now. Don't worry I am in control. I don't know our culture that much but I will try."

"This your culture thing seem bothersome...."

"It's sweet. Just that the white people have made it sour but never over here. You will see something before you go."

I felt good because Dora was talking to me in a very good and loving mood. The scenes got my attention again

"That's a nice scene over there. What's that... what's that...," I kept pointing to different locations.

Don't get lost in your memories. That's the beauty of Kumasi. You will be excited of everything you will see because you are in a different world.

"How old is this city?"

"Why...?" I think it's older than New York or Philadelphia and of course Washington, D.C."

I sighed within, trying to make sense of what I know about Africa and its jungles and the funny characters in the movies.

Why didn't someone show us some of these things in the books or on the television," I asked.

"There is time for everything. It doesn't matter now. I brought you here to learn things by yourself. We are simply a proud people because as Africans we have every reason to be proud because we have our culture.

She waited until we got a better view of what I was excited about before answering me.. She took her time to explain to me what was going on in the valley. On the left where I first pointed to was the central market which was as big as a four football parks joined together with rows of assorted roof colors over the shelves.

"This is the focal point for most commercial activities in Ghana and some West African countries."

"Wow," I retorted.

"We have to go home now; but on the left is the Kejetia Lorry Station. All cities and towns in Ghana and the neighboring countries shop here daily. You can see that my city is unique in many ways."

"Is the small booklet the man gave you becoming of any use to you?" My wife, who knew I was lost in my imagination asked.

"I'm seeing more than what I can explain. That's why they say that experience is the best teacher. You are a special person," I said and attempted to kiss her. To my surprise, she moved away from me.

"I told you," she said. "No kissing in the public over here. The moral codes is highly respected over here. I am aware of this but sometimes when I am in the mood I forget myself.

We joined Stella and helped a taxi driver who was patiently waiting for us to come back. Just about fifteen minutes, the driver stopped by a house, and many people came out of the house to peep at us. I could hear nothing but "Akwaaba! Akwaaba!..." They hugged, shook hands, stomped on their feet and some came out almost half naked, according to my moral standards. I became amazed because of the structure and design of the house. While Dora was gaily mingling with her people, l admired the set up of the house. That structure could contain more than hundred family members an d was built in such a way that there would be no room for individualism. They all had a common kitchen, a common water supply source, and common bathrooms or toilets.

It was like Dora was the only visitor in the house. At first I didn't bother, recalling what happened at the airport, and continued to enjoy their welcoming spirit. I guessed Dora became aware of my thoughts, seeing exposed breasts, because she kept looking at me.

"Don't worry, they will pretend that they do not know you, but everything will be fine." Dora whispered in my ears

"The dilemma is started again," I murmured to myself.

Stella came to me and led me upstairs to a room. It was like an apartment with two big rooms where our entire luggage was kept.

"My sister will be back soon," she said and then left the room. Soon after she left there was a knock on the door.

"Come in," I said. Dora entered, followed by three women. I smiled even though I did not know what was on their minds. All the women looked alike. Both of them stared at me. Dora said something in their language; they frowned. I hated this scene. Then she spoke English to the other two.

"This is Jason, my husband... I wish you will let mommy understand this." They kept silent for a while. "Jason, these are my mother and sisters." She pointed to the mother first then the sisters. There was a long silence. There was no word to describe their countenance. I quietly pondered over Charles's advice again. I should grow out of these cultural shocks and hope for a happy end.

"Who is Jason?" questioned the mother. It took Dora quite a while to respond.

"Mame, she just said 'my husband," the sisters, said simultaneously.

"Your husband? He is an Afro-American." There was a prolonged Uh! sound echoed among the sisters.

Suddenly, the mother looked directly in my eyes and spoke several words in her dialect to me in a serious but not a mean tone.

"Mame, Americans don't speak Twi... they speak English," said Stella. The mother quietly turned to Dora and expressed her concerns.

Why didn't you tell me you were married to an Afro-American? He doesn't speak our language and I don't speak his language either.

"I don't like it and you are the first person to do this in the family."

"Mame, don't be too difficult. It will only take him three months to learn the language, if that is the problem," Dora broke her silence.

"I hope you will let him understand that I don't have anything against him personally; I love him because his people are part of us but the Ashanti culture does not coincide with what you are doing." Stella then entered the room unnoticed and leaned on me.

"I wish my wife is bold like you." I murmured to myself.

"My father wants to see you all," said Stella. At this time it was like I wanted to shit on my self, I mean, if the mother, was so displeased with the situation who knows what the father would do?

Dora signaled to get prepared to meet the family. I peeped through the window to see what was going on in the yard. It was like a crowd in a theater. I had to hold on tight to my composure to prevent me from panicking. The mother left us alone and I took the opportunity to change into a very gorgeous Dashiti outfit which Dora bought for me. She reminded me again the proper way of greeting the people–it starts from the right to the left and I had to shake hands with everybody.

"My mother is not a problem right now."

"We have to convince my father because he paid my way through school."

Our marriage doesn't look too good right now. Before I could say anything, we were called to come to them. We wasted no time to answer to the call. Descending on the stairs of the two-storey building and all eyes raised up to look at you was mind bogging. Dora was led by two young ladies while a gentleman led me. We moved in a single line.

"Whatever he does... do the same," Dora whispered to me. They started from the right to the left shaking hands, just as my wife had oriented me before. I could tell that her family was happy to see me in that Dashiki attire. Dora followed the two ladies while I was right behind the man. We were just shaking hands without any verbs but they were making sounds like "yeemo." When we came to the middle, the man removed his shoes and lowered his cloth off from his shoulder before bowing down to greet the man and the person sitting next to him. I did the same thing with the exception that I could not remove my dashiki. After greeting them we sat in a row on reserved seats. Someone said something in their language and most of the people stood up and shook our hands. Some of them said aqaaba others would say to me yo are welcome. After the greetings, they gave us choices of water and soft drinks.

"Every thing you see is a part of our culture, just hold tight . . . you will be okay," she whispered in my ears. Moments later, someone shouted from among the crowd.

"Agooooooo!!

"Aameeeeen!" the people responded with one accord. The place became as quiet as a graveyard. We were in the center of everyone's eyes

"You are the one that traveled four years ago to the overseas country. Can you tell the people why we are gathered here today?" the spokes man spoke in English. I was very happy about the question. She remained silent for a while.

"We have not heard anything yet. You have to tell us." The spokesperson repeated several times. I can't tell whether it was a trick or she just could not answer them. To my dismay Dora started to cry. For whatever reason, she did not tell the stately gentleman that she came to introduce me to her parents.

"Dora just told me to tell you all that she came in peace and in the name of God and that she completed her schooling before coming." The man changed his tone of voice and informed the people that Dora has something important to tell her family but she needed more time to think about it." The spokesperson surprisingly changed his tone.

"Kofi!" the father called for someone.

The person came forward and the father asked him to take me home until tomorrow. While the man Kofi was leading me away from the house the people dispersed.

Dora quickly took me upstairs for my luggage. It was like she wanted to cry but she patiently explained to me that we needed to be separated according to the dictates of their culture.

"I am not worried about my father. I can take care of that. What I worry about now is where you are going." I nearly fainted at that moment. I had to sit down and she wiped the sweat on my forehead.

"I am going to be slaughtered?"

"Oh no don't be crazy," she said with a smile. "My worry is that the man has a beautiful daughter in the house who behaved almost like a prostitute," she concluded. My fears subsided.

"The whole area would be watching you and if you make any mistake to be a victim to her sexual maneuvers, then that would be used against us to stop our marriage." Honestly my wife was right about that because any father would not tolerate that from any son-in-law.

and why do I have to go there in the first place?" I asked

"You see, in the African world, a girl cannot introduce a boyfriend or husband to be direct to the parents. I have to give him that respect," she said. "Even though my mother and my sisters know about you, my father pretends that he had never heard about you. Somebody else, not me, had to do the formal introduction."

"Who will do that then?" I said.

"Leave that to me."

"How many times will she keep telling me don't worry....?" I murmured to myself.

Chapter Five

Twenty minutes later I found myself in another house. Mr. Kofi"s house which was smaller than Dora's place but I could not figure out which one contained more people. I was given a well furnished room. Kofi took his time and explained to me that it wasn't easy to marry from that family and he would see to it that Dora would sneak into my room during the night. I was kind of suspicious about his plan because of what Dora told me about him.

All that I needed was to lay my wearied body somewhere so I could concentrate. I was resting in the comfortable wooden bed--recollecting my memories reflecting my encounters. Within about fifteen, Kofi's daughter came in without knocking. "My name is Mercy, Kofi's daughter, I understand you are our guest. You are welcome and good luck," she said. I could not keep my eyes away from her. She appeared like the daughter of the Greek goddess, Aphrodite. She was beautiful, charming and an angel in a perfect body. She could not withstand my gaze on her. She brought me something to eat-water, rice and corned beef stew. The food was well seasoned and delicious. After meals I contemplated that at least I would see her once again to check out her beauty. I don't mean to make any approaches because if I dared do anything like that, in spite of Dora's warning, that would be a disastrous doom. Within minutes, during my serene concentration on Dora and Mercy, someone knocked the door. "May it be Dora, Mercy . . . ?" I murmured. I found it hard to believe that it was perhaps Dora. Yet still my feelings started streaming within me.

"My brother, hurry up . . . our father is waiting for you," said a voice. I wondered who else it might be.

"Who is this again?" I asked. I reasoned. The voice was the voice of Mary, the lady I met at the Embassy. I tried to reposition myself.

"Open the door. This is your sister." Mary's voice became clearer and echoed through the door. But why is she calling me brother?" I wanted to open the door immediately, but there was one small problem. While I was lying on the bed hoping to see Mercy again, I mean just to eye again without doing anything, my thoughts kind of went deep into romantic evolution and in the process of having these romantic thoughts, comparing Dora and Mercy, I got lost in my imagination. It took some time for me to be able to come to the door. Mary Nkrumah became impatient as her knocks became louder and louder.

"Hey! Jason, what's going on in there? Is everything okay?" When my feelings subsided I opened the door for her.

"Oh Mary, you are here . . . ," I said.

"I have heard all that has happened. Your wife's older sisters have told me everything. You don't need to sleep in this house. My family will take over and do whatever the culture demands for you to do."

She came with her brother to help me to carry my belongings to their place. We drove in a Mercedes Benz to their place. Wow! I loved their place. It was big and more gorgeous than Dora's place.

"How old is your house?" I asked.

"Why? My grandfather built this house long before my father was born," she said. My father is about sixty five years old now. You can figure that out yourself." My previous knowledge about Africa is gradually becoming a fallacy. I know why Dora did not answer my previously questions. She took me to a room on the second floor. The room was furnished with a brass and gold platted bed. This really blew my mind off for me to sleep in such a bed in Africa. I like it here but what is the motive behind me being here? Is it a trap or a conspiracy? Back in the States, one of Dora's friends told me in confidence that Africans could snash away peoples husbands with ease. It might not be the husband's fault they have a way of doing that. The advice revisited me and I tendered not even to trust Mary Nkrumah and her family. I became terrified. I needed to talk to Dora but there was no telephone nor did I know anybody who would run an errand for me. I temporary became insane and could not reason anymore.

Tiredness overtook me and just before I dosed off I heard someone knocking my door. I had to guess who was behind the door. While debating within me, whether the person might be Dora, Stella, Mary or perhaps Mercy I heard a male voice. That voice was strange to me so I opened the door. Three people entered including Mary. I calmly asked them to sit down and gazed my eyes on Mary. I guess they expected me to do or say something pertaining to their culture, but I just gazed at Mary.

"Jason, this is my father and that is my mother," said Mary. I shook their hands with feelings of a great inner joy. The father gave me a special smile which helped to brighten my countenance.

"Paapa and Maame, this is Jason, the man Dora brought from abroad," said Mary. They shook my hands and ended with akwaaba (welcome).

"My daughter had told me everything. In this society no son in law will dare approach a would be in-laws to request to marry their daughter,"

"But Paapa he is not from here?" said Mary.

"It doesn't matter whether he is from Buckingham Palace or Addis-Ababa, Ashantis will never let their culture go for anybody. Your wife is polite and aware of the culture that's why she did not dare to introduce him to the parents directly."

"But why was she crying?" Asked Mary

You must be a thinker, don't let your presence at that foreign embassy divert you from your way of life as an Ashanti," warned the Father. Their deliberations were not in my favor but beggars have no choice so I had to condone.

"Do you want to eat anything? We have tea and bread," said the mother.

"I am alright," I said shyly. I think she was just kidding with me. Momentarily, a girl brought in a jug of hot water, tea bags, can milk and bread on a brass plate.

"It's late now so eat something and go to bed. We will talk later," said the father and they left.

Within twenty minutes I ate the bread and many cups of tea to fill my stomach. When I quenched my hunger I laid down in the comfortable bed.

I had a sleepless night because I did not know what to expect next. I still have not ruled out about any double motives of Mary. I dreamed about Yolanda talking to my mother; about me and Dora doing it in the hotel room, and briefly about Mercy. About five o'clock in the morning, as usual in this place, the cock crew. I woke up from my dreams and looked out in the window. Coincidentally, I saw Mercy strolling down the street as if she was looking for somebody. She was decently dressed and staring around her while leaning on a mango tree.

"Damn! This girl is beautiful...," I grumbled. I nearly committed myself by waving to her through the window. This was the time I wished I was in the States. I would not have let such a beautiful chit to go free.

Mary came to my room, about six o'clock in the morning and led me to the bathroom to bathe. Unlike the bath set up in the hotel, where one had to stand up to bathe from a bucket of warm water, I had to sit on a stone seat and my legs on a foot stool. It was comfortable, sitting down to take a warm bath from a silver bucket. Now I realized the true meaning of a bath instead of showers. They have no showers nor hot and cold water faucets. After the bath I dressed up and instantly I was called to my adopted father's room. In the room were Mary and her parents, two young ladies, and a boy of about twelve years. The father asked all of us to have a seat and listen carefully to what he was going to tell us.

"Mary, where is George?" asked the Father. Surprisingly, before Mary could say anything the man entered and all of them said simultaneously, "here is George," after George was welcomed to the house, the father told him why he asked for him and he was there to be a witness The father took him aside for a private consultation. The last forty-eight hours had been a whirlwind of eye opening. I have still not known my fate. "When are we going to Dora's house?" I murmured to myself. The two men returned with smiles on their faces. George came and shook hands with me. "You are welcome," he retorted.

Finally my father spoke some magic words.

"George let this young man know that I will marry for him but before that he must realize that I have adopted him as my son as long as he is in this country." George got up and stood closer to me.

"What is your son's name?" he asked. The family conversed among themselves for a while

"His name would be Jason Kwame Bonsu. His slave name is Washington but we do not need that here.

"Jason, your father has accepted you to be part of this family so your family name would be Jason Kwame Bonsu. Be sure to use that name wherever you go. He is doing so because Dora's family does not marry their daughters to just to anybody. We must hear from you first before we go forward," said George. I stood up and knelt before my father.

"From now on I do not have any father but you. I am leaving behind my slave past... may God bless you," I vowed.

"You are a respectful child. From now on anything pertaining to your wife and family leave it unto us. When we go to the house don't talk because you do not know the culture.

"In his country they can take someone's daughter to the court and pay money for a married certificate," Said George. They laughed about this for a long time. I did not see anything funny about it.

"Krakye (gentleman) you cannot do that here," said my mother. I have been hearing this word Krakye, for educated men and Awuraa, for educated females. They say it so often as if it's part of the English language. One of Dora's sisters came to the house carrying something, covered with a white towel, on her head. Mary got the load from her and took it to my room. The sister called my father aside and informed him something. I was asked to go to my room to eat my breakfast.

The sister brought some breakfast, some fried eggs, bread, tea, butter, and sugar. "After all this is not a big deal since Dora has been allowed to send me breakfast." I murmured to myself. I enjoyed the food. Just before I finished my plate George entered my room. I love to be around him because he speaks English fluently.

"Krakye don't finish all your food. Leave something on the plate. Here men do not wash dishes so you have to leave something for the kids who will wash the plates for you," said George.

"I am glad to know that," I said. He called the young boy, by the name Kumi to come and take the left-over food from the table. He then informed me that Dora's father was very angry at Dora throughout the night for her decision without their knowledge. Sadness overwhelmed me instantly.

"So what does that mean," I asked.

"Don't worry. It's not your problem anymore. We will take care of that. Do you have some cigarettes?" asked George

"No, I don't smoke but you can send the little boy to the store." I gave him a twenty dollar bill. He looked at it and smiled. "God bless you," he said.

By ten O'clock the next morning, it was time to go to Dora's place and my duty was just to follow them to wherever they went. When we arrived, there were about twenty-five people gathered in the house already. They sat in a semicircle with Dora's parents in the middle.

We shook hands and this time I was perfect in the greeting style.

After the greeting someone stood up among the crowd. Luckily the spokesperson spoke in their language but George interpreted everything in English to me. The cultural bargaining then began.

"Well Opanin Kwasi Bonsu, you have come to us this morning and we welcome you with these," said the spokesperson after presenting some drinks to my father. Everyone was given something to drink. My family thanked them for the drinks.

"Opanin Kwasi Bonsu, you are the one who has come to us this morning. May you now tell us what brought you to this house this morning?" said the linguist. My father stood up and the house became quiet.

"Okyeame (linguist), let Opanin Kwasi Yeboah and the family know that we are here this morning with good news," said my father. (The people grumbled among themselves).

"This young man, Kwame Jason Bonsu is my son who has just come from the overseas country."

The people grumbled among themselves, some of them talking loud in their language. Mary and my mother were also talking to them at the top of their voices.

"Agooooo!, shouted the linguist.

"Ameeen!," the people responded at the top of their voice and silenced immediately after that.

"Your story is very interesting," said Dora's father.

"I am serious, don't take me for a joke," said my father. "I joke a lot but not this time. I would have been mourning for seeing my son had it not been because of your daughter." George whispered in my ears "don't worry, this is how the people relate to each other."

"Opanin (elder) I know you are not joking but what has this young man who you claim to be your son is doing in this house?"

"First before I answer that question I want to explain my point.

"Go ahead, Opanin, we are listening," said the spokesman.

"Everyone here in town are aware that my great grandfather's son was captured by Babatu and sold him into slavery. Even though it was a long time ago but you all know that our family members are easily identifiable when you see them." Dora's family excused themselves for a few minutes. I enquired from Mary about what was going on but Mary could not give me any reasonable answer. She simply told me that I should not worry for father knows what he was doing. I kept my fingers crossed. I had not seen Dora yet and I began to worry until Stella came and stood by my side. I bent down and asked about Dora. "She is in the room crying," she said softly. I stamped my foot on the floor hard. My mother screamed at Stella and said something in Twi (their language)."

"Brother, control yourself... here is not your father's country. You are lucky her parents are not here. That would have made things difficult." moments later the family arrived and had their seats.

"Okyeame (linguist), Let papa Kwasi (referring to my father) understand that this family is not interested in their family history at this moment unless he has something that is related to the matter at hand," retorted Dora's father. Instantly, my father stood up and vividly addressed them.

"We are serious. We are not fabricating. I am here to ask your daughter's hand in marriage for my son here. In the first place I thank your daughter for bringing my son home." My father went straight to the point and I was anxious to know what would be next. My father, with his face looking serious, addressed the people that it would be in the interest of everyone in the two families to understand him. He asked me to stand up. He pointed to my forehead to reveal the grey hair at he tip of my forehead which I always try to cover it. I did not want people to think that I am old but it is becoming an issue now.

"Oye (is he) a Banie (one with white birthmark on skin or hair)?" Dora mother asked. She leaned to Dora's father and whispered something into his ears. The father frowned.

"We have seen that... anything else?" Dora's father asked.

"I was told to move about two steps forward. Father raised my left arm and they witnessed a sport of my skin about one and half inches diagonal. This is something about me that I have been able to keep secret. Another commotion started again among them. An old lady who has just entered the house started crying when she saw the gray birthmark. This is something

I have been worried about since my boyhood days. Playmates have been making funny comments about my birthmark but it is becoming something significant at this crucial moment. I recollected the day Dora questioned about this gray patch on my forehead

"There are some people in my hometown who have this type of hair." At that time I didn't want to hear anything about the Africans and the Afro-Americans having anything in common.

"Opanin Kwasi Kra, is your son, according to the dictates of our culture, fully prepared to ask for my daughter?" The father asked. "My family made some movements and around them. My father stood up and signaled for me to stand up by his side also.

"Okyeame...tell Opanin Bonsu that we appreciate her effort to educate her daughter here and abroad to study. According to our tradition, we came with our initial kokooko dowry with these: two bottles of schnapps, two cases of minerals (soft drinks), fifty American dollars to the father, twenty dollars to the mother, and fifty dollars for the brothers and sisters in the family."

The spokesman stood and stretched himself up as if she wanted to be taller than his height. That prompted a short span laughter. I prayed that the next step would be a dream come true for me and Dora.

"The spokesman presented the gifts and the money to the family." The family confessed among themselves. "Where in the world can this happen in order to get a wife?" I questioned myself. "The dowry is even insignificant. If I had known I would have given them more money to shut them up. Why did Charles told me it will cost a lot of money?" I debated within me.

"Let Opanin Kwasi Kra understand that, the family would hold on unto his dowries (first bridal gift) and they will hear from me later," he said. The people began to dispearse.

Chapter Six

By accepting the first bridal gift there was some hope that the parents were considering my request. I decided to tour the city to get exposed to the social and the cultural life of the people. My younger brother Seth volunteered to take me around the city.

The first thing I learned, while I was out there mingling with the people, was the use of the feet as a major form of transportation. Everyone was walking. Seth walked very fast and I had to double my steps in order to catch up with him. From Ashanti New Town, the part of the city where we lived, we came to the edges of the central market located in a valley. I could see the roofs of the shelves and all around the market were hundreds of people engaged in various economic activities. Even it was unbelievable to see what was going on outside the market and on the roads where pedestrians, vehicular traffic and vendors shared the passage ways. To me the whole scene I had seen so far was nothing but congestion. I refused to enter the market when Seth suggested.

I cannot compare this place to the world where I came from because life styles are just opposites.

With these scenes I concluded that Africa is a different world. I have never seen so many people sharing a little space like this in my life. People could touch you, step on your feet, push you or anything that could be done but no one would say 'excuse me.'

"Let's go somewhere else. I can visit the market later," I said. We walked uphill. He asked me a series of questions about the city and when I could not answer any of his questions, he was surprised that I did not know anything about the city.

Seth stopped by a building with different and strange architectural designs and the roofs were made up of little cones. Seth asked me if I had seen that building in my book before.

"We don't have pictures of Africa in our books. I think it's a castle where the King lives...," I said. He laughed. You have not seen this in your history books. I thought you are an American."

"No doubt about that."

"I live here but I know everything about your country. Our geography teacher is very good about that," said Seth. I was really ashamed of being ignorant about this place while this small boy knows more about other cities from their books. Nobody had ever taught me the geography of Africa.

"I can see that you are smart and need to go to America. I will take you with me."

"This is nothing to me. We learn everything about the world in our geography class.

"What about this building. It looks different from the other buildings," I tried to change the topic. I pointed to the same building. That's the Kumasi Fort...," he answered. I had wanted to know more about this particular building but I had to be diplomatic about my ignorance. "It's too late for me now,' I whispered to myself. Seth started telling me the significance of the Kumasi Fort. He narrated that the place was a hideout for the British soldiers when they fought the Ashanti army. I could not get the history. I couldn't reason how the British army was able to build a fort in the middle of the city at the time when the slave trade was alive. I could not just figure out He wanted me to say something but I never learnt anything like that in school. He looked at me and frowned.

"Follow me," he said and started walking. We walked around the fort and entered through a gate guarded by a military officer.

"What's this place?" I asked quietly.

This is Kumasi barracks, the home of the soldiers.

"Please let us go back. I don't want any troubles.

"They won't do you anything." Luckily he listened to me and we walked away from the military base.

"Do you know about Nana Yaa Asantewaa?" This time I wanted to tell him that we needed to go home. I nearly shed tears. I realized how deep I had been mis-educated and how privileged I am to have such a brilliant brother to patiently show me the city. My wife could not have done a better job than Seth.

"You have no tribal mark on your face," said Seth when he looked at my face.

"What's a tribal mark?" He laughed. "Do you know if any of your people were slaves?" I asked. He looked at me as if I was asking a stupid question. He hugged me with no apparent reason. Our people don't talk much about slavery here. Most people lost family members to the slave trade. He stared at me and then stoop to the ground" I think you are the one from our family, that's why my father adopted you." I could not give any answer. I really did not want to go into that topic again so I drastically changed the topic and moved away to a different place.

Five minutes walk from the Kumasi Fort, we found ourselves strolling at the back of a building that seemed to be the most beautiful structure in the city. All fences are made up with flowering plants including rosy flower buds that scented the atmosphere. While I was enjoying the smell and the elegance of the tropical clean atmosphere, a nice looking lady, in a long blue dress, quickly emerged from the building.

"Seth, what are you doing here," she asked. I could not help but to stare at her beauty. She had a radiating countenance like the beauty of the gods. I could hardly look in her face.

"Nothing, I am just showing him around," he said.

"This man is older than you and what can you show him? You need to go home and read your books, "said the lady and then entered the building.

"Who is she? She is beautiful," I asked Seth.

"That's my sister . . . my father's daughter. She is a nurse at the hospital.

"I see. So this is a hospital?

"Do you like her? I can talk to her for you."

"Oh no I am part of the family now. He gave me a strange look. I wondered why he did so but I could not ask him.

"That's true I forgot . . . you look like us. How come . . . ?" I could not answer his question which revealed that as much as the Africans in the Diaspora do not know much about Africa so also the Africans knew little about them. I changed the topic.

"So what's this building?" I asked.

"This is the famous Okomfo Anokye Hospital,..," he pointed to the signboard.

"Who is Okomfo Anokye?" He became so amazed about that he stopped talking for a while with his arms folded on his chest.

"Oh buoy!" he said. I wondered why he said that. We do say 'Oh buoy' in America, and I quickly realized a possible link with this expression and our African ancestors. But I reserved any conclusions until later.

"What's wrong...?" I asked

"What school did you attend? You came here with Auntie Dora and she never told you anything about Okomfo Anokye?"

I was wondering within me why I should know anything about this person. I needed to study the war of the States, the constitution and democracy in relation to the cold war to pass my school exams. There was no time to study anything about Africa.

"No, I spent most of my time trying to woo Dora to be my wife." He strangely looked at me.

"Dora is going to marry you; are you sure?"

"Why not... what's wrong about that?"

"The white man has a proverb: 'Look before you leap;' Dora's uncle is the chief."

My case was getting more and more complicated. I read in the dictionary about Kings and chiefs but I never actually understood their functions in the society.

"So what does that mean?"

"What...?" I thought it wise not to commit myself to be naive. I did not want him to remind me about that I knew nothing about their culture. "Perhaps this is the part of the marriage plan... to test how much I knew," I grumbled to myself. Luckily he changed the topic.

I looked in the middle of the four walled concrete walls that we sat on and I observed a sword–which looked very ancient--pricked in the ground. I became curious but I could not ask.

"Have you read that in your books? He asked when he saw me looking curiously at the legendary sword.

"I don't think so," I said.

"That...," he pointed to the sword. "That's the Okomfo Anokye sword."

"We never studied anything about Ashanti. What more is to be said about this sword?" I grumbled to myself. I looked at my brother in the eyes.

"No," I said. Before we could say anything a group of school children, came over and surrounded us. The teacher started telling the pupils the history associated with the sword. Now Seth did not need to ask me any more questions about the sword and godly sent man in the name of Okomfo Another. The teacher pointed to a short tree or shrub a few feet away from the sword and instructed them that Okomfo Another cursed the tree that it would never grow more than four feet and that tree is still alive. Again he took them to a palm tree a few feet and showed them some foot marks on the palm tree that was left when the man Okomfo Anokye climbed the tree. He told them that Okomfo Another died in 1740.

After the school children had left a few questions were left unanswered and I had to get the answers from Seth or Dora. I decided to ask Dora for her to know that I know some of their history.

Seth's step sister came out again from the building. She came over to me and extended her hand. "My name is Akosua . . . welcome to Kumasi, the Garden City of West Africa," she said.

"Thanks. I am Jason from America . . ." She moved back and rolled her eyes with a big bright morning smile.

"You don't look like an Afro-American," she said. "You look like us."

"She is Auntie Dora's husband," said Seth. She instantaneously frowned. She stared at me as if she just saw me for the first time. Her mood instantly changed.

"I wish you good luck. An Afro-American wishing to marry this man's daughter, I wish you the best of luck," she said and then walked away. I became confused about her remark. We ended the outing and walked almost half a mile to the house. Before reaching the house I had already thrown away three wet handkerchiefs that I used to wipe my sweat. My body was burning like fire from the hot tropical sun.

Two days later, my father informed me that–according to the dictates of the culture once the family had accepted the first dowry, Dora could come and spend the night with me.

"You cannot do that . . . leave it to me," he said. I smiled and we hugged each other. He left the house that evening and behold when he came back Dora was with him. She never said a word to me. She went straight to the bed room. It was like heaven had fallen on me. I lifted her up and threw her soft body on the bed. I had the opportunity to be cozy with her once again. We made love before talking about anything else. She told me everything the family planned to do. She said that her father cannot refuse to honor my father's request but the next obstacle was her own family members in the village. She was very serious about this but my mind was not on her people again. I was all the time on her, caressing, telling her how beautiful she was.

"Let's put the family mess behind us ... I may die trying to understand your people. How many families do you have anyway?"

"I am glad you asked but it's not in my position to tell you. Let's forget about the topic but don't forget to ask your daddy tomorrow." We continued to make love and slept soundly throughout the night. I surprised her just before the cock crew with a question about the Sword. She was very surprised that I knew about the legendary sword.

"You are learning fast. The man commanded that no human being can remove the sword from the ground."

"Such a special thing in a Black world ...how come we do not see it in our books. Everything about Africa is primitive ... ," I murmured.

Early in the morning, one glorious Saturday, Dora got up as soon as the cock crew. She won't do anything with me anymore. Before she left, she asked me to shower before talking to anybody in the house. I understood that it was part of their culture.

"Africans are something else," I murmured to myself. "Who cares whether we made love or not?"

Chapter Seven

Two days after the sightseeing in the city my mother came to my room and conversed with me in private. The people are just full of love, family oriented and treated people with a special tourch. I wondered what she had to say to me.

"My son I know you are like someone swimming in the ocean without eyes. You are just battling against the waters. You are battling against the culture which you know nothing about."

"It's true that I am so naive about what is going on around me, but now I appreciate the efforts of you and Papa." She moved closer to me and held my hand. I became cool.

"Let me tell you something the marriage consists of four stages. You have gone through one which is just to open the door to the next phase," she said. "That is, if the father accepted the kokooko dowry in good faith."

"Then I think the first one is very important because I can sleep with her. That's all I need." My mother laughed about my comment. "Aborofo suban (white man's character). It's not like that over here. The first part (kokooko) means that you are telling the parents that as of now if they can't find their daughter they can approach you for her where about.

"So when is this going to end after we have gone through all the necessary rites? "Everything will end in Dora's home town where the people have more power over her." My joy started to subside away. She revealed to me that both the second and the third part may take place in Dora's hometown since she is from a royal family."

"So if I don't finish and I decide to go home what would happen?" My mother padded me on my shoulders.

"You are just a little boy. This is Ashanti, you know. If you do that Dora will be given to another man and you or she cannot say anything. This land is 'parents' powers forget about the white man's way of life.

"What am I expected to do?" I asked. Before she could answer, my father came to the room and asked her to leave me alone.

"What are you telling him?" asked my father. She quietly left the room without saying anything.

This is the time I really reasoned that I should have listened to my parents and peers instead of coming to Africa to blindly swim in this ocean of cultural blockages. I would have married anybody, besides Yolanda, among the many girls I dated before meeting Dora. I would have avoided this marriage ritual involving every member of the family.

A few days after that Dora's parents sent a messenger to the house to talk to my father. I was in my room when my father came in and padded me on my shoulders.

"My son, there is good news. The family had accepted your first bridal gift. It means a lot. Inferring from what my mother related to me I was curious to know more.

"Is that the end . . . ?" I asked

No, they say we have to go to Dora's parents for the rest but the good part is that they cannot prevent Dora not to visit you. That was all that I wanted to hear. I jumped for joy and started dancing. I kept saying me-- *da ase, me da ase* (I thank you, I thank you . . .).

Soon after that Dora came to the house and repeated the good news to me.

"My father's side of the family has agreed to your request," said Dora.

"My Father just told me," I said.

"It's not over yet. You know we are matrilineal, now we have to confront my mother's side of the family," she continued.

"What does that mean? This thing here is too adventurous."

"My only fear would be the response of my seventy-year-old conservative grandmother . . . ," said Dora.

"That's a good news for us. The old ladies won't worry about what young people do."

"You just don't know. They hold our cultural Bibles and interpret it without any flip of the tongue. Any way let's pray for the better."

"I am sure that we will be able to go to my village next week," Dora predicted.

Both father and mother had warned me to be very careful since the marriage is not completed yet. If I did anything stupid against the norm the parents can use that against me.

"We are not telling you what to do. Just be wise and careful," Dora advised. I just did not understand at all.

It was Dora who explained to me what they actually meant, that we should be careful not to let people know that we have sexual intercourse. We could be together but could not touch the apple. This is the rule that both of us could not be able to honor in our privacy. My only intention was to pray that she becomes pregnant before we leave Ghana

Though I don't attend church regularly yet I forced myself to pray to God hoping for a miracle to happen while I was in Africa.

"Father God, you know I have come home to root in my ancestors home… have mercy upon me in my quest to have a wife from the motherland. Teach me to learn more of my ancestral roots, Oh God. Teach me to understand the culture of my ancestors, both here and abroad. Let my hopes for a cultured wife be fulfilled in your name."

I prayed one morning at five o'clock. On that faithful Friday we began packing. I was very skeptical since I did not know what to expect in the living conditions in her hometown. I just had to follow her judgment and plans. She packed two suitcases and a few bags stuffed with many assorted things: clothes, toilet rolls, napkins, canned foods and many others I could not even name them.

"What's all this about? Why are you packing all these . . . ?" I became curious.

"You are not in America; Africa will always be full of surprises. More especially anything pertaining to marriage in Africa is the most complicated and longest journeys ever to be taken," she said. I have vowed never to argue with her once I am in her country. By eleven o'clock in the morning, we found ourselves at the city center, Kejetia Lorry Station, to chatter a vehicle to her hometown. It was about noon and I had the opportunity to observe the people's way of life with scrutiny. I saw the statue of a woman holding a gun as if she was in a war front. That statue inspired my attention and I went closer to read the inscription Nana Yaa Asantewaa, leading the Ashanti army to fight the British in 1900. My brother Seth, during our outing introduced the Kumasi fort, the wonders of Okomfo Another and the hospital but she never mentioned about this woman. I have disciplined myself not to ask many questions because I have learned a lot through observation. I took many pictures of the statue. Dora promised to buy me a history book that will explain everything about the history of her people. What came to my mind was to compare this woman with Harriet Tubman who lived about hundred years apart from each other. Both fought to liberate their people. My memory began to roam between the two worlds with sadness I walked into the road. When the driver blew the horn I became disoriented and threw myself unto the side walk. I nearly fell into an open gutter. Unfortunately, I turned over the table of a vendor. My wife became embarrassed about this and had to apologize to the young lady, who was selling oranges.

"Why are we here? What are we here for?" I asked my wife. I had just become confused.

"I know you are confused about our way of life. Remember these vehicles here have no insurance nor are there any lawsuits in this country."

"You don't mean it."

"The act of suing people was not introduced by the Europeans into our societies. They knew better that our culture would not warrant such misdeeds. Don't worry about many things. Your first priority is to get a wife from among the people family." I loved this moment because my wife was conversing with me with an open mind as if we were in the States where no culture bonded us together.

While we were talking, a nosy woman overheard our conversation.

"You might be an American . . ." said the lady. Dora replied her in their language. She stared at me.

"It's nice to see an Afro-American here. Most of them are Ghanaians you know."

"You see how much we love you over here; I wish you do the same to us in your country." My wife's remark was unacceptable to me but there was nothing I could do. It seemed that I was in a school of Patience and Tolerance and I needed to obtain a pass to return home with a wife.

"My eyes are opened now and we would do better to educate our people at home," I said. She looked at me and smiled.

"Where are you taking him?" asked the lady again.

"To the village," answered my wife.

"Who is he . . . a researcher?"

"No."

"How do you know? These people come here behaving like the sheep in wolves clothing, to investigate everything we do. You are just a young lady and you don't know what you are getting yourself into," said the lady in a clear British accent. My wife looked at me and smiled. I was surprised that the lady had changed her tone.

"You are not going to say anything?" asked Dora. Having known that my wife wanted me to express myself, I tried to convince the woman that I wasn't a spy for I came to the country with my wife. I held Dora's hands and hugged her. She shook her head.

"Really . . . you married one of them?" said the lady. My wife just smiled and patted her on her back. If smiling were to be money, all the people here would have been millionaires. I just love to see them talking and smiling simultaneously."

I wish you good luck with your people," she said and then departed. We have been standing at one spot for twenty minutes with many activities going on around us. To me it was strange and interesting to see hundreds of cars, lorries, big vans loading and unloading goods and passengers at the place they called Lorry Station. I was very astonished by this experience to be among people of all walks of life, having one common goal, rushing to get to their destination. To my surprise I learnt that some of the passengers and cars came from other countries–Ivory Coast and Upper Volta just to buy goods for their various markets. I asked my wife why she took me to the lorry station instead of charting a taxi to the village. After all we could afford the cost.

"What taxi? We are traveling in one of these vehicles. You have to experience what it takes to be an African by mingling with Africans to know the difference. That will help both of us in our relationship. I know everything about you and your country and you have known the same about me." She gently hugged me and removed a particle from my forehead.

"You have really shown me a world different from the chemistry class," I said while kissing her on the cheek. She kissed me back on lips. "Not even that. The situation the white man has placed you in. . . . he transplanted your ancestors but I am going to transform you with my culture . . . "

"I am just arriving from Atlanta, Georgia; you will not get it like you have it at home, said a young gentleman in a three-piece suit. She just heard my wife and I conversing and he quickly poked his nose into our conversation. He did not like my looks and moved away without introducing himself.

"My own people come here from overseas behaving like the white man, wearing suit in this kind of weather? I have already wet six handkerchiefs with sweat."

"They Just want to show that they came from overseas . . . to get women's attention."

"I see . . . perhaps I should have dressed like this gentleman among all these beautiful women." I mumbled to myself. After a while I became restless. I decided to move away from Dora to mingle among the people. I could not believe I could ever be among hundreds of black people in the center of a city, where there was no white man and managing and directing their own business and personal affairs with an exception of a few Asians, I presumed some Indians and Lebanese people.

I came across a beautiful, sexy young lady in the station. I could not help it. She was sitting behind a table decorated with assorted colors of ladies underwear and bras. I sneaked to talk to her while my wife was not around. She was very attractive and immediately I fell in love with her. She told me the price was ten cedis each. I picked up five pairs of the ladies underwear she was selling and paid for it. She produced the most beautiful smile on her face. I gave her one pair back after I gave her more money than the price she asked for.

"You can have it," I said. She smiled and started speaking in her language while giving them back to me. Later I learnt that she could not speak English. I became very disappointed. I just waved my hand to wish her good-bye. Suddenly she shouted, "Kumi! Kumi . . . !" My brother-in-law had just come to the scene looking for me. Luckily Kumi did not pay her any mind and we walked away. I was very happy about that because I did not want him to tell Dora what I did.

"You bought something?" Kumi asked, after seeing the bag.

"Oh, yes . . . something private for my wife."

"Why didn't you call me . . . how much is it," he asked.

"Ten cedis for each." He thought I had given my money away for nothing. He left me and went back to the lady. I became scared because of what I did. Luckily he informed me that what I bought was actually worth five cedis.

"Make sure I am with you before you buy anything from here," he advised me. "This is a bargaining city..."

She is my uncle's daughter," said Kumi about the girl. I didn't say anything again, entertaining the fear that she might be one day mention it to Dora. "Where have you been? The vehicle is about to leave," she said.

"I am sorry," I said without disclosing that I was lost among the crowd.

"I know you are excited to see things for the first time. I hope you will write something about the good things you see in my country when you go home," said Dora softly in my ears.

I gave her that assurance. We boarded a twenty-two-seater Mercedes Benz van. The front seats were reserved for Dora and me; Kumi had to sit at the back with nineteen other passengers. The driver was a dark complexioned and a stout man who kept shouting 'Boma! Boma!" until someone told him that the car was full. We left the city about two o'clock in the after noon. Sitting at the front seat, I had the opportunity to see the scenes in the country. About five miles away from the city we had left the city and passing through small villages, tall trees, people walking everywhere on the road sides, heading toward their homes or villages from their farms or from nearby towns. The driver habitually blew the horn and the people on the roads and in the villages would wave their hands. This is the time something hit me. My memories shifted back in time to when I was in my twelve-grade class. The teacher showed us a movie about Africa. In that movie, animals were roaming about in the jungles. The teacher explained that lions were carnivorous and Africans and other animals were their prey. I remembered mocking at an African female student in one of my classes and even nicknamed her 'Jungle Girl.' We embarrassed her so much that she had to withdraw from the school. I could not understand. I wished Kumi were the one sitting next to me so that I could have had some answers to quench my curiosity.

"Where are all these wild animals and snakes people talk about in the States?" I leaned and whispered in her ears. She frowned.

"You tell me," she said. "All that I see on the roadside are villages, towns, farms, trees and the farmlands."

"What!" Kumi shouted from the back.

"Nothing! Dora screamed at him. Dora then started explaining to me what she wanted me to know the life of the people both in the cities and in the countryside. An hour later, the driver stopped at one of the large villages that had a big market and a small station for passenger vehicles. As soon as the vehicle came to a stop, vendors, as usual, surrounded the vehicle. I was surprised to learn that everybody bought something from the vendors. I was just watching these people and thanked my God for giving me such an opportunity to be among people of such a high dignified culture which we have ignorantly degraded in my country. Dora bought about seven loaves of sugar bread and shared the seventh one among the passengers

"What are all these breads for? You want to be constipated?"

"I don't even think this is enough. Wait and see. These things you see here have been going on before even your country was born. These structures were built by your ancestors who went to America and the West Indies."

"Dora where does your husband come from?" asked a young lady who was selling boiled corn on the cob. Dora replied her in her language and the young lady smiled. She gave us some of the corn without asking for any money.

"Oh Auntie Dora, you are back?" another one screamed from behind. She forced herself inside the car to go with us. Later I learnt that she was Dora's niece.

After twenty minutes the journey continued on. Even though it was only a twelve-mile journey but the activities on the road was so much that I felt like I was traveling a hundred miles.

"From Washington, D.C." Dora answered

. . .and he is your husband? . . .something is not right," the driver commented. "You educated folks want to turn our world upside down."

"Don't be nosy. Is she your daughter?" intervened an old lady at the back. The driver reminded the mate that we would reach our destination within minutes. The mate collected the passenger-fares from everyone. Dora paid our fare with ten-dollar note and told him to keep the change. The driver then smiled at us.

"Thank you . . . you're alright with me," said the driver.

When we arrived at Boma it was like the whole village was on the street to welcome us. "I just kept saying to myself 'Africa is beautiful, Africa is beautiful;' the unity, the bond between the people was just too much. I can't explain why many of them spoke to me in their language. I just replied them by knocking my head especially when I heard the word akwaaba. We were escorted to Dora's house.

Surprisingly, Dora's house was very outstanding among all the homes in the village. Most of the houses, to me, were like huts. They were mud walls with little windows that were not professionally made. Dora's house was cemented all around it and contains more rooms than any other structure in the village. She gave me a little warning about how to behave.

"This is my maternal family; at Kumasi you met my paternal family and I hope this will be our last stop. Be careful here because this people here have more control over my marriage affairs since my children would belong to them," she said.

"Why is that?" I asked. She looked at me.

"Don't ask many questions about what we do and the logistics behind it. The culture is like a constitution, obey without questions." She joined the crowd and left me standing alone. Instantly I got to know what it meant to be a stranger in a foreign land. Since I wasn't part of the welcoming extravaganza, some ladies led me to a room on the second floor.

"Your friend will soon be back," they said and left. As usual my curiosity always kept me going. I admired the room even though it was not as cozy as the rooms in Kumasi. I admired the wood that was used to make the bed. It was as shiny as the glass with its matching furniture. I lay on the hard bed without springs, and hoped for the next positive action. I questioned within me why my adopted family did not come with me. I know if I had asked Dora she would have answered me with some cultural excuses again.

About twenty minutes later, Dora entered looking exhausted and sweating. She started changing her clothes and with this short privacy we had I made sure the door was looked and for five minutes, whatever I did with her body and mine, was an attempt to make her pregnant. To have privacy in her country, with all these extended family members around is like trying to chip a stone with your nail. No sooner had we separated from each other, someone knocked the door. Within thirty seconds, we got dressed and Dora opened the door looking as holy as the virgin Mary. The family wanted to meet us. For the first time, she gave me a full assurance that she was fully behind me and even if it became worse she would override her people's decision to marry me.

"God forbid. God forbid that it will come to that disastrous level," she concluded.

"Why do I have to go through all this? You are my wife." She laughed.

"This is the real Ashanti stuff, different from what is spoon fed you in your text books which is nothing but an attempt to destroy Black dignity." Within a short time we were ready to face the family.

Chapter Eight

It was like I was temporary insane when I went to meet the family, with the grandmother sitting at the center stage. What kept my sanity was Dora's previous promise to be on my side even if the family turned against me. Dora had given me a prior warning about her grandmother. I was just to listen to whatever she said and agree. Immediately the grandmother set her gaze on me, she called me her grandson and started talking to me when she knew that I was an Afro-American.

"All our people were taken away including my grandmother's oldest son. I understand he has a family over there... do you know them?" she pointed her stick toward me. The interpreters quickly narrated what she said.

"No," I nodded. She continued to lament how she missed him and wished they could come back home.

"She is a symbol of our family history. If she dies, we will lose a lot of our history," Dora whispered in my ears.

The grandmother rather entreated the family members to treat me with respect and as a member of the family.

Please let no one try to marry him. His great grandparents might have been taken away from this family," she warned the family and then walked away I could not clearly understand what she was saying, my interpreter was, perhaps, not telling me everything she said. While I was doubting about what she was saying, Stella came to me and whispered to me; You cannot marry Dora, grandmother said so." The people heard Stella talking to me and shouted at her.

"Get off from there... you are too grown." Stella moved away quietly.

"They are joking; they can never get Dora from me," I began talking to myself. Dora went and helped the old lady to walk to her room.

It was like I was living in hell at Boma. The people advised Dora to reconsider her decision; the marriage, even though the parents may have agreed to it, couldn't take place without the final blessing of the old lady. Those who were in favor for me to marry Dora informed me how they had been persuading the old lady on my behalf, to give her final blessing to us.

During the second week, I felt more or less than an outcast, who was totally rejected by the family. Ironically, without any explanation, Dora ordered more of our things to be brought from Kumasi to the village. I became more afraid than ever but she never told me the main reason for her action. After the things have been brought back to the village, I had an idea of wearing my sport clothes and join the children to play soccer at the school park. But my idea was shattered shortly, when I was informed that father wanted me to return to Kumasi without delay. My heartbeat tripled, and my mind became blank. My wife knew the mental state I was in and she entreated me to relax in the bed with a soothing kiss.

"Everything is going to be alright," she said.

"But I felt like I was being deported . . . shipping me home . . . ," I said without thinking.

"So you have not passed the test yet?" she said with a beam of smiles on her face. "Now you know how it feels to experience what your people had been doing to foreigners?." At this moment many thoughts came to my mind. I remembered my friend's co-worker at a fast food store, who was arrested by the immigration officers and deported him for working without legal papers. I felt guilty for the part I played by laughing at him. Now I felt the same way, leaving my wife in an African village; I wondered what all that meant.

"So that's why you are shipping me home," I said.

"Where is home? This is your home," she said with a smile. "This is not an exit with no return. I promise you will return to complete the marriage initiation. I really became confused about the whole ordeal.

"It seems to me that I am going through some rituals . . . ,"

"Rituals . . . ! You have not seen anything yet. This will prove to you that you are getting an ideal woman, not those types of women you pick up from the streets or night clubs for dates." I could not challenge her for this kind of a thing, No brother would be able to go through all this ceremony before getting a sister to marry.

Just before I left to answer to my father's call, Dora convinced me not to worry so much because the grandmother would eventually give her blessing to our union.

I reluctantly agreed to go. While we were out there waiting in the dusty street, passing through the middle of the village, curiosity abounded in the whole village and many others wondered why I was leaving. Someone strangely touched me from my back. I didn't bother about the touching because Africans torch each other; even males hold hands while walking together. But my wife giggled. I wondered who that person might be. I turned around and behold, there stood a slim tall white lady behind me. It was like a dream; It was my first time ever getting that closer to a white woman. It was like: should I kiss her, hug her, shake hands with her or I should just ask her who she was. I quickly turned around to see Dora's reaction but strangely she had disappeared. She had left me there alone with the white lady.

"Can we have a little walk?" she asked. I was stunned to death.

"Okay!" I said, with the hope that Dora was just tricking me with this white woman who sounded like an American. For ten minutes, I could not even look at her face; I thought I was dreaming. She knew what I was going through and she patted on my shoulders. She kissed me on my cheek. I heard hissing sounds around me; the children were musing about the kissing.

"Don't put me in trouble . . . this people here are different," I said softly. Before she could tell me whatever was on her mind, a six-year-old girl came over to us and leaned on her.

"Teacher Amma," said the little girl. "My uncle wants you." She did not want me to have a heart attack from my incessant doubts. She had to introduce herself.

"I know your anxiety. I am a Peace Corps volunteer. I teach these children."

"But you are different from them . . . they like you?"

"Very much . . . here they regard people as people. They know nothing about our discriminatory mess at home."

"I realize that. Since I have been here."

"They do not understand what is called color." This place has changed me for the better," she said. It took a while before I could speak again.

"What do you teach them over here . . . ?"

"That's an interesting question ... here the teacher teaches all subjects for each class during the year... the system the colonial masters designed for them."

"But why did she call you Teacher Amma?"

The children do not call adults by their names without a title, or rank. The first thing they asked me, when I first came to this land, was the day I was born. Once they knew the day I was born, which fell on Saturday, they have been calling me Amma."

"And you like that ... ?"

"Yes. It sounds better than my own name; any way my name is Bravasky Gunterville, from Boston, Massachusetts." I became relaxed very relaxed after conversing under a mango tree. Both of us could help laughing when three mango fruits fell on us almost at the same time. "No winter here so the trees bear fruits all the time," commented Bravasky.

"I see, I also observe something, the birds are high up on the trees, and they are beautiful with assorted colors," I asked.

"You are very observant. Over here the birds have plenty of fruits and seeds to eat in their own natural environment. Secondary, they are afraid of humans because they kill them for food. All the fowls you saw in the city, such as the vultures, the crows, the English bird etc, they a re not eatable. We have been talking without even introducing myself to her. When I looked up I could see a crowd of children who were curiously looking at us from a distance.

"My name is Jason Washington, I reluctantly boarded the van and introduced myself.

"That's nice. Everything about you is Washington." She began to tell me that I have a wonderful wife but she is born into a rooted culture that she herself could not come out of it but to obey the elders.

"I have already seen enough since I came here ... "

"You have not seen nothing yet but if you overcome then you will see how humane these people are ...," she intervened. "I will do my best to assist if I am around."

Our conversation ended abruptly when Dora appeared and informed me that the van was ready to take me to Kumasi.

"Damn! This girls is deporting me ... ," I reacted by stomping on the ground. Dora and the white lady just laughed at my behavior.

"I am sorry...," I apologized.

"Honey everything will be alright. Just be mindful how you behave in public because the whole community is watching you. I can't defy their decisions." the children had brought all my luggage, to be ready to go to Kumasi.

My wife whispered something into the white lady's ears. Both laughed and clapped. I was really kept in the dark and I looked for Stella and Kumi, in order to have a hint about what was happening to me, but they were not around.

I reluctantly boarded the van and bid them farewell with tears in my eyes. All I could see was the white lady and my wife conversing and smiling. A scene of a white woman and an African talking and smiling in such closeness of heart as if they were equal on the African soil was a beautiful felling. Both of them waved 'me goodbye' while the van was disappearing from the scene.

"If a white person has been able to make it, then it would be a shame if I fail in my quest." I murmured to myself.

From Boma to Kumasi, we had a lot of fun in the vehicle. The driver was very jovial. Almost every passenger could understand and speak English so he spoke English most of the time. If I had not gone closer to Africans, I would not have known how they think and behave. One joke that got everyone laughing was: A farmer raised a boy and gave him all the wisdom he had so that when he died the boy would continue the legacy with the future generation. The boy went to the white man's country and added the white man's wisdom to his head. This means that the young man might have two heads. Unfortunately when he was coming to his village from the white man's country, he forgot the head that the father prepared for him and brought the head with the white man's wisdom. The young man entered his father's house and started saying Hi! To those who had gathered in his father's house to welcome him, he began kissing the people, and then referred to his father as George and the mother Grace." end of joke

"Do you know what happened?" asked the driver. The people continued laughing.

"The father ordered that the young man be put in asylum until he gets his original head from those who stole it."

A joke like this was heard throughout the journey. Because of Seth I got the messages the jokes portrayed. Now I realized why my wife taught me how to greet the people especially the elders and the chiefs.

Just before we reached Kumasi, Seth and I got into our little conversation and I had to do all the explanation. At first, we talked about the schoolteacher.

"The school teacher is a White American and I am a Black American." I told Seth, to answer a question.

"You are a Black American? I thought you are an Afro-American?" he interrupted my trend of thought, proving how both of us are ignorant of each other."

"It means the same," I said.

"I see, Americans always use big words or slang. To my surprise many of them, who were not natives of the village assumed that I was an Ashanti.

"Where are you from. . . ?" the young lady sitting next to Seth asked me in the Twi language. How I wished I could speak like teacher Amma. I looked at her without saying a word. She frowned and asked Seth if I was a "Manfrani" (a word I later learnt that it meant anybody who is not an Ashanti). The complexity was too much to grasp. Seth broke the silence and announced that I was an Afro-American who came for a wife. There was a long period of silence. I waited anxiously to hear what was going to happen next.

"No wonder you are interested to know more about Americans. His wife must remember to bring her head home . . . when she goes to America," said the driver. "My man, it's all a joke, we love Black America so you are welcome home." I was relieved with his good humor gesture.

The conversation and the anxiety ended abruptly as the van pulled into the crowded Kejetia Lorry terminal in Kumasi. We had arrived in Kumasi. I gave Seth five dollars to buy as much bread as he could for the children. Before we took a taxi home, we did a little sightseeing of the market. We went closer to the central market and gave him my little binoculars which I had on me.

"Tell me everything you see over there," I said to him. He never understood what I meant. He was not used to using real binoculars.

"You're just like the white people . . . they are always holding some of these in their eyes when they come over here."

"That's what it was made for," I said and then got it from him for a brief demonstration. Before I could finish, we were surrounded by children of Seth's age, who curiously wanted to know what Seth was doing.

"I see everybody . . . very close in my eyes. We don't have to go there." Seth became excited.

"This is mine . . . I can walk about with it like the white man," he requested in advance. I got the binocular from him and then had a closer view of the market. The first view I saw was two market women exchanging words and suddenly broke into a fight. To my surprise the people were just standing around, some of them laughing, until some elders came and separated them. While I was enjoying the scene Mary Nkrumah appeared.

"We don't have much time left. We need to go home as soon as possible. You can do your sightseeing later." We went inside her car and went straight home. In the house the people came and hugged me and as usual, they showered me with the word 'Akwaaba, Akwaaba . . . This time I know the response to Akwaaba from the village, so I greeted back to them Yeemo

"My father came and hugged me and shouted in my ears, something like yaady nconim '(Yadi Nkonim)! How I wish I could understand and speak the language like teacher Amma. I became quiet trying to understand but they won't interpret it. "Dora deported me from the village," I whispered to father. For the first time I experienced my father laughing humorously. Everyone asked what was going on with him. He said something in Twi and the whole house became a laughing scene. They hugged me and some said 'don't worry' and others danced around.

"We won," he said. "Dora is now your wife, after we fulfill two more conditions and then get approval from the queen mother." I smiled and hugged my father, my mother, my sisters and my brothers. We were about twelve in the family.

I shook everyone expressing my happiness. "Say me daase (I thank you)," instructed Mary. I repeated after her, Me da ase Papa, me sda ase mame, meda ase Mary etc etc. They laughed at my accent but clapped for me for the attempt. After that, I inquired to know, now that it was imminent to get my wife, what I had to do, to marry my wife for the second time. They looked at me and laughed. My mother came and tapped my shoulders. "Son, you will see what our ancestors could not take with them to your world. You will see the beauty of our culture in marriage and you must take it back to your people. "

I was in deep thoughts imagining how this traditional wedding would be like, one of the sisters came in the house with the biggest broom I have ever seen. "Oh no, not again," I nearly went into coma. This was the moment I remembered the practice of jumping the broom in black history, when our ancestors had to jump over a broom in order to be pronounced married by the master.

"Not again!" I yelled without reasoning.

Everyone stared at me.

"I am sorry, I didn't mean to distress you. The broom just reminded me of my history."

"You're not living in your history anymore . . . what can such memories do to you now that you are bathing in the big ocean of Africanity," said my father. "Put all those histories behind you." Now I could feel the pride of being African.

The presence of this broom was a mere coincidence with my mother's mentioning about their ancestors.

""... my son what's wrong about the broom?" My father later came to me about this question. I had to tell him the little I know the slave masters' slave marriages.

"It was good for the slaves. The white man did not invent that for the slaves. We do not do that in this culture but some Africans practice it. It has a lot a meaning. I was astonished to hear that from my father, giving praises to the practice of jumping the broom. To me broom is nasty to be associated with marriage. My father called all the family members together and asked us to hold our hands. He stood in the middle, holding some straws.

"I want you all to listen."

"All tribes in Africa are the conglomerate of the African Ancestors in the Diaspora and jumping of the broom was a practice of some of the tribes," commenced my father. I really had to interrupt him.

"But the broom is a nasty thing to use . . . nobody like that broom concept in America."

"Broom! What about the broom . . .to sweep the compound?" asked my brother Seth who had little knowledge about the history of black America.

"Papa, you need to explain yourself some more. I can't comprehend what you are saying.

"My children the broom consists of many symbols or beliefs. The jumping of the broom of the slaves was honoring and respect to the African ancestors."

"How?" asked Seth

"The straws of the broom, joined together represent the family, the handle that is held to sweep represents the

Almighty God and the ribbon, tie or rope that bound it together represent the lobe, unity, enduring one another in all their married lives." After father had finished his lectures, nobody could utter anything. We just did not know and luckily this culture does not practice the broom culture; I was kind of justified.

"Even thought we do use the broom in our marriages but it is usually mentioned during the marriage counseling. It is a symbol of coming together of both families and the commitment of both families. That's why it would not have been easy for you to approach Dora's family alone without your family. I hope you understand this now," contributed my mother. From this moment anything associated with jumping the broom evaded my mind.

We had to return to the village within a week to fulfill the rest of the rituals. At the moment I was the only one who was left in the dark. The rest knew what was going to happen when we go to the village but none of them, not even Seth, would tell me anything. Our father instructed that from that time no one should correspond with me in English. They had been speaking the Twi language to me and I had to force myself to understand by following the body movements, especially with the movement of the hands.

Two days before the time to go to Dora's hometown, three co-workers from the embassy, including two white ladies, arrived from Accra. Mary had invited them to come and witness the Ashanti cultural marriage (aware). When I questioned Mary why she brought the white ladies, she explained that

Ashanti marriage ceremony is so unique and language oriented that foreigners don't get the opportunity to witness and understand it because of the language barrier. The embassy employees took the opportunity to witness the first cultural marriage between an American and an Ashanti lady (awuraa).

"I love you...sister," I said while leaning on her.

"I want to show you something." She got up and asked me to follow her. She took me to a room where things were laid out like a small warehouse.

"Oh, you have a store?" I asked. She laughed.

"No these are your dowries to your wife."

"Why, do I have to give all that?" I asked in my ignorance.

"Yes. Dora is no cheap woman. Somebody educated her to the University level. Yo have to prove that you deserve her golden apple."

Wow! It was like the son of a famous king marrying the daughter of a famous queen. I have been hearing about some people giving dowries during marriage but I never dreamt that it would be applied to me. Everything that could be given to a loved one, some of them strange to me though, were presented as gifts to my wife. To me most of the items had nothing to do with marriage but when I questioned she told me to wait and see and never to question the culture. Someone knocked on the door. It was a man who had come to deliver something to my sister. She gave me the parcel to open.

"It's just for you... and your wife." I could not believe they could be rich like that to give us gold wedding rings.

My mother was right when she said that Ashantis sit on gold and wear much gold at their functions. As she advised me to bring some gold I can show her that I came to the gold land.

My sister advised me not to worry too much for Africans have their own way of life. I was getting interested in what my father had to say but mother interrupted. She said something in their dialect and both of them went behind the house. They came back to inform us that we would be going to Boma the following day. When tomorrow came a Mercedes Benz bus was parked in front of the house. Everybody ran helter skelter in the house to get ready.

"The driver is here. Pack all the stuff...," repeated our Father

"Go and get all your stuff...," Mary commanded.

"What's going on? I asked.

"We are going to Boma. We are going to perform the final customary rite and after that Dora will be your wife without any more restrictions."

I quietly entered my room and with the help of Seth I packed all my things inside my briefcase. I was first to get ready to go inside the bus.

The driver's mate packed all the things on top of the van. He covered it with trampoline, a waterproof fabric, and tied it up with a rope. There were about twenty five of us in the van.

The young ones were sitting on the adults' laps.

Mary, father and I sat at the front with the driver. On the way my father coached me about what would be expected of me and what I should do.

This driver was not as funny as the first one. He appears to be a serious minded individual and well versed in their history. He told a lot of history about the Ashantis. But in all his historical episodes he never talked about the slave trade.

Just before we reached Boma, I guessed, they wanted to build my spirits up with songs. They sang nothing but the plantation songs. The voices and the style they used to sing those choruses were obvious. I could not believe I was in Africa, especially songs like:

When the Saints Go marching on and John Brown's Body... They sang with singleness of heart until we reached the outskirts of the town. About a few hundred yards to the main street of Boma, I could see the crowd standing in the center and gazing at our vehicle. But for some reason, father asked the driver to stop

"I am giving you my last advice. Be very careful. I am going to try to force this marriage on your behalf but the parents still will have the final say."

"When you marry Dora, you must remember that she belongs to her family, not you nor your family."

"Don't hesitate to take me to America...," said one of the girls whom I learnt was one of my father's children from another wife. The driver also opted to say something.

"A husband is like a driver, sitting in the front seat, you should know and understand how to drive a woman. Sometimes they behave like galloping horses, but you must learn how to be patient with them. They hate usage of force," contributed the driver.

"When you go back home tell your parents that they belong here and they should come back home. I have plenty of land for them. You can't be part of this world when you don't own a land," concluded my father. I became confused. It looked like we are starting everything over again.

"Why do l have to woo the parents again after all these money we have spent?" I murmured within me.

"When you may not see your wife today," Mary whispered in my ears.

"Don't say that," I replied to everybody's hearing.

"Stop the nonsense, Mary. What did you tell him?" said my father.

"Nothing, I am just playing with him." This made me smile but I was still dwelling on papa's advice.

Finally we touched the main street of Boma and the driver blew the horn loud and continuous. Many people came outside and waved.

The driver stopped in front of a big concrete house with its walls painted with symbols and different types of drums. It seemed like the whole village came outside either with curiosity or to help us to take our things inside. I was dazed about where I was and what was going to happen next without Dora. Isn't scary to go inside this strange house?" I debated within me. Seth came to me and whispered in my ears.

"This is our palace (chief's house)." Before I ask him why we were there Dora appeared, wearing a gorgeous African outfit.

"Wow, what have they done to you . . .as beautiful as an empress," I adored her.

"I am glad to see you in good spirits, wow you are beautiful."

"I am too . . . what's going on?" I asked.

"Nothing . . . just a normal thing. Don't worry," she said. The driver's mate brought down my luggage and my wife quickly got my luggage.

"I am going home with you?"

"This is not America. You should always be careful of your in-laws. According to the culture you have to be away from me until the whole thing is over."

"What thing?" I asked.

"What are you here for?"

"Me or we?"

"This is my town. I was born here. Why are you here?"

"To marry you," I said reluctantly. She moved closer and hugged me. My father saw us hugging and then demanded my attention. We went inside. The palace was very big with about fifteen rooms. I was given my own room. From this hour they had given me a name in their language. Everybody called me by that name. I never knew it was me that they were referring to until Kumi came to my room and briefed me on a few things that transpired while I was away.

"What does Ayeforo mean?"

"You need to learn our language before you go to America... it means bride or bridegroom. I have been calling my sister like that too."

"Tell me something... while I was away... what happened?"

"I can't tell you," said Kumi.

"I thought you love me. You see my brother tells me everything."

"Who is your brother?"

"Seth...," I pointed to him in the yard.

"That's auntie Mary's brother.

"I know auntie Mary Nkrumah is my sister too." He laughed about it. I guess he did not believe me.

"My grandma did not want Dora to marry just anybody. They wanted her to marry Oppong Duncan." As soon as he said that my intestines twined within me.

"What kind of a thing is this...," I murmured to myself. Someone saw Kumi in my room and quickly asked him to go away from me.

"I told you, I can't tell you everything. My father will whip me for that." He walked away. Everybody was busy doing something. Later I found myself sitting next to the chief in his chamber with my father, sister and the chief' spokesman. Still saddened about what Dora's brother has just told me. I became moody and a little bit absent minded.

"I will be in support of any man from abroad interested in my subjects simply because this village lost five of our men to the slave traders. We believe you are the first of their offspring to come home to us."

"Oh God it's me oh, have mercy upon me oh, wipe away this slave stuff away from me, let the final outcome be good for me!" I was praying like crazy within me. I was very worried about the chief's statement and I wondered why they have to report this to the chief instead of the Dora's family.

"What we will do for you may encourage your people to come back home," said the chief to his linguist.

The linguist repeated the same thing statement to me in English. He called one of his wives, after he said that, and spoke to her in their language. The woman came out with something wrapped in a white handkerchief. She was instructed to give it to me. The woman politely moved to me and handed me the handkerchief. It felt heavy in my hand. I became afraid thinking they wanted to put some voodoo on me. Everybody was sternly gazing at me.

"Open it," said the linguist.

"The white man came to Ashanti land and enriched himself. In the same token we do not want you to go back home poor," said the chief through the interpreter. I opened the handkerchief with haste and behold, it was a pure diamond. I nearly dropped dead. I could not believe what I saw. At this moment I entertained the thoughts that I wouldn't care anymore if I didn't marry Dora.

I showed it to my father. They all bowed to the chief and thanked him for his precious gift. Mary instructed me to do the same thing they did.

"Say 'Nana me da w'ase (Nana I thank you),'" she demonstrated to me

"Nana me da w'ase," I said. No sooner had I said that than all of them clapped their hands amid much laughter.

"I want to be part of the tomorrow's ceremony, so be here about two o'clock," said the chief. He got up and went inside his chamber. My father asked Mary to keep the gift for me.

"You will never understand. This is part of the culture. This is the chief's contribution to your wife to support your marriage ceremony tomorrow," said Mary.

"Can I see my wife tonight?" I asked.

"You may do so after tomorrow, when you have proved yourself as a husband," she said and then went away with my diamond.

I hate to be sleeping alone but I had no choice until Dora finally becomes my wife. I could not sleep that night. I was awakened several times by horrible dreams of killings, fights and forced labors of certain groups of people. When we woke up in the morning, everybody asked me how was my night. I wondered why they were asking me such questions but I dared not say anything. My only interest was to have the marriage stuff over with and be able to go home with my diamond. The idea of Duncan Oppon never left my conscious mind. Could it be that I am being deceived with this diamond in order to buy my love for Dora in order send me back to somewhere I cannot proudly call my motherland. No, this cannot be true. I know my Dora will never another man besides me because of the way I have I wish I would know what my wife was going through with her people. I have enough with the chief and Kumi, positive and negative forces

This experience was too much for me. We had to wait for the time the chief set for us to meet. All of us who came from Kumasi slept in the palace except the women who stayed with the chief's wives. At one o'clock in the afternoon, the palace became crowded like a dancing hall. I have heard about drums, but what I experienced this afternoon blew my mind away. Two men came to the palace and opened a room full of drums of assorted sizes, colors and designs. Some of the drums were about six feet tall. The drummers started drumming and within a twinkle of an eye, the place was filled with the people from the community. I think some of them came prepared while others were asking the people about what was going on. That was my happiest moment, watching the people dancing to the tune of the drums, to see men and women jumping up and down, communicating through body movements, of their hands, heads, legs and the eyes. I could not find the right vocabulary to describe the beauty of the scene.

"This is what the white man should have shown to us instead of the Tarzan swinging on the trees," I murmured to myself. While I was enjoying the drumming my wife and her entire family entered. I saw my wife in a beautiful white cloth, decorated with jewelry of all kinds and sizes. I had never seen her with that heavy smile on her face. I wondered what she was happy about. While the people were entering and taking their seats, a young beautiful woman beckoned to me.

"Go to your room until you are called, else Dora's brothers will come to pinch and scratch you. It's part of marrying someone's sister," said the young woman. I had wanted to face the challenge to be part of the culture but I respected the lady with a silky long hair and her advice. Later Dora sneaked into the room. We kissed. She was in tears, for what reason I don't know. We wore the same outfit. Mine was a big flat piece, about eight yards.

"Do you know this ceremony will cost over $3,000?"

"Where is the money coming from?

"Ask your god family," she said. "Be careful of my brothers. They have planned to embarrass you, unless they get a sufficient share of their part of the dowry."

"From whom?" I asked.

"You. Have they not told you what you are supposed to do?"

"Not a thing...," I said.

"I hope you don't embarrass me and yourself." Having said that she left me. I wondered what would happen next. The drummers started drumming with a different beat and suddenly the place became quiet. I walked around the room, trying to get comfortable in my African attire. Lots of thoughts came to my mind and I weighed the whole adventurous ordeal. In fact if I had known what I had to go through perhaps I would not have bothered to marry Dora. Suddenly, I heard a knock on the door. Seth and Kumi came inside and asked me to follow them

"I am not going to let my brothers do anything to you," said Kumi.

"What do they want from me?" I asked. The boys laughed.

"Don't you know about 'Akonta gye sekan (brother's share of the bridal gift).' said Kumi. Now I am really tired of the culture and wanted everything to be over with.

"Don't you realize that he is not an African . . . he doesn't understand that?" said Seth. I never said anything to the boys. While I was walking down on the steps, the people clapped for me. I guess they admired my outfit. I was directed to where my adopted family was seated. I sat in between my African father and mother while Seth was squatting in front of me. My family and Dora's family began communicating with each other mostly in their dialect. Teacher Amma arrived within that time to boost my spirit up.

"Teacher Amma Akwaaba. (Welcome)" She was warmly welcomed by the crowd.

She rushed to shake hands with Mary and her co-workers, two of whom were white ladies. All the Americans and Mary stood behind me.

My father brought a lot of drinks, gave some to the chief and the elders. After they had finished their type of prayers and drinking, they commenced their usual welcoming-ceremony. Thank God, I did not have to talk. My father took over when the interpreter asked him to tell them the purpose of our visit. My father stood up and removed his sandals and lowered his African outfit below his shoulders.

"Nana Kyeame (linguist) Let Nana (chief) know that we came here this morning in peace. I did not come here for a bad cause but a good one. Today my son has asked me that he is now a man and have met the daughter of Kwasi Yeboa and Akua Selina. Both of them met in the white man's land. My son here is one of the great grand children of my great great-uncle who was captured into slavery. Dora went there and met him, has married in the white man's way and has brought him back home. We are here to ask you, the ancestors and God's blessing to allow my son to marry the daughter of Opanin Kwasi Kra.

At this point the crowd intervened with various hissing sounds that I couldn't describe. The drummers started drumming briefly and the women sang to the tune of the drums. My sister interpreted some of the songs sang by the women.

It is only the mother

Who knows what her children want when they cry? Come back home, come back to sweet Boma

The white man (Kwasi Buroni)

My eyes started shedding tears and some of the women actually cried with tears for a reason, I did not know. The sad moment was brief and quickly died away. The drummers changed the whole atmosphere with a different drumbeat. The house became silent again.

The interpreter cracked a joke.

Papa Kwasi we didn't know that you make American babies too. When did you go to America to have a child?" Everyone, including the chief laughed. My father had already told the chief everything. Papa Kwasi replied back with a joke.

"I sent for his mother and made this baby out of her. She went back and never came back. It's now that he has come back looking for me." The joke quickly died out and everyone became serious. According to their tradition, whatever is said in a public gathering like this the linguist has to repeat what was said. He interpreted what Papa Kwasi Manu, my adopted father had said.

"... Bonsu is asking for the hand of Kwasi Yeboa's daughter in marriage. His son and your daughter met in the white man's country." The people grumbled. I was curious to know what would happen next. I looked around; I could not find Dora nor Kumi and Seth.

"Agoo!!, the spokes person called for silence.

"Amen!" they responded and the place became as quiet as the graveyard.

"Papa Bonsu the family has heard you. But you're aware that Ashantis do not believe in educating our women but Papa Yeboah had endeavored to educate her daughter both here and abroad. You know that's a lot of money that he spent to educate a girl instead of getting married and increase the family's population. In this regard, how do you prove that your son will be a capable husband to both his wife and the entire family...?" said the linguist.

Those supporting me communed among themselves

"Nana, please give us some time and we will prove that we did not come here to joke...." said my father.

Suddenly the drums echoed again for some kind of announcement. A middle-aged woman, who was dressed in a gorgeous outfit with gold ornaments worn all over her, and the homemade sandals that she wore were adorned with gold dust. An entourage of young girls led her. The person in front of her was a man who carried a stool, besmeared with gold trinkets, which was carved in the shape of an elephant. Now I had understood why Seth once told me that the chiefs sit on gold. Her presence demanded attention from everyone. All but the chief stood up and bowed for her. I loved her gait and the way and manner she waved her right hand to greet the crowd and sat next to the chief. I learnt later that the highly respected woman was the queen mother of the village. She addressed the crowd in their language and nobody gave me any interpretation. When she finished speaking, the people started murmuring among themselves again. It seemed that some of them were kneeling before the queen and begging for something. The mother left her seat into another chamber. "I thought everything is over for me," I questioned myself.

Later I was summoned to go inside the room to the queen. This is where it got on me and I even regretted for following my wife to Africa. How could anyone in my world ever believe that a woman who supposed to be a legal wife cannot cook for you, kiss you before parents, gives the love that is supposed to be for the husband to the entire so called extended family and above all sex is like a taboo for both of us? It was too much for me to bear at this time. I reluctantly entered the chamber where I found Dora sitting before the queen mother. My wife was not looking happy either and that comforted me a little.

"What is going on now?" I whispered to her.

"I don't know yet, honey, we have to go through some cultural hurdles."

"Dora where is your husband from?" asked the queen mother.

"A..meri..ca..," she said. I like this conference with the queen mother because she spoke American English. That might be an opportunity for me to express myself and to tell her how much I loved Dora.

"Dora how old are you?"

"Twenty three."

"How old were you when you went to America?"

"Nineteen."

When and where did you have your first menstrual period?" Dora found it difficult to answer this particular personal question. It looked like she was guilty of something. I don't blame my wife because the questions were too personal and the answers were none of her business. She leaned on me and sighed.

"Perhaps we can't get married."

"What is this?" I jumped up uncontrollably like I was losing my mind.

"Control yourself honey and face the cultural bridge cannot be taken lightly. It's the constitution of the state written by our ancestors. You have to understand this today. What I say about this marriage would be final and you may take your marriage certificate back to your home," said the queen mother.

I could feel from their reactions that it was not going to be easy. Dora shed tears and wanted to leave. I held her tight.

"Are you betraying me?"

"You have to do something to win her heart since she is speaking English. The queen now turned to be lenient and asked me to sit closer to her. She talked to me in confidence with the language that I understood. I learned that she lived in my country for three years and unfortunately she was forced to exit to avoid forced removal.

"There is no alien in Africa; your country lady, Teacher Amma, is not regarded as an alien. She is part of us," she said and then leaned back on the person standing behind her. I could not give any better response than to let her know that Black people have nothing to do with what goes on in the leaders minds. She just laughed and then turned to Dora. She blamed her that she failed to report her first and second menstruation to her as their custom demanded. But since she has been living in overseas she would be forgiven.

"I didn't know that . . . this is strange to me . . . it's not my fault."

"I don't blame you. Foreign influence has misplaced some of our cultures." She turned to me and assured me that she has eradicated all cultural restraints because of me. She turned to me and stared at me.

"A cultured wife is better than wives without culture; I have a special love for you and your people in America and I have the hope that you will go home and tell your people what you have experienced here."

"Will you like to go back to America again . . . ?' I asked. She frowned and leaned back.

"For what? No way. My position now is more than your president. I sit on gold and I rule until I die."

I realized from her that she would never work as long as she remained the queen mother in the town." I was really enjoying the queen mother but the drummers started drumming again.

"They need me now. Your marriage ceremony will start soon. I have told them to go ahead but remember, this woman," she pointed to Dora. "She is not a slave and never treat her like a slave. You must respect her and worship her." We got up to leave.

"Thank you very much," I said.

"Say Nana Hemaa meda wo ase (Nana I thank you)," Dora padded on my shoulders and kissed me on my cheek. The queen giggled. I repeated after her, "Nana Hemaa me da wase."

"You are doing a good work to teach him to speak the language," she said. "I am not supposed to speak any other language in public. I just wanted you to understand this aspect of our culture--that's why we talked privately. The linguist was called and he led all of us out of the chamber. Dora was taken away from the crowd. When I sat down, my people patted me on my shoulders. The drums and the music echoed again when the queen mother joined them. She signaled to the linguist.

Chapter Nine

"Ago!" Shouted the linguist. "Amen!!" Responded the crowd and silence abounded. Everybody positioned themselves in their respective places.

"The queen mother Nana Akua Asantewaa, has given her final decision that the marriage between Dora and her American-husband can now take place," announced the linguist. The crowd responded; some people with joy and some of them mumbled. The linguist then turned to my family. He looked directly at me and spoke in a simple English language, "If you want a wife, it's now time for you to demonstrate that you are a man who is ready for a wife."

My father patted me on my shoulder and advised me to remain calm and watch the next stage 'the ceremony' I wanted to see my wife at that moment to have a glimpse at her dimples if only she was as happy as I was. But the whole ceremony was blanketed with culture. She was hidden away from me. When I asked to see her, I was told that even though the way was opened for me to marry her but she is not my wife yet.

To my surprise, a gorgeous lady, almost about the size of my mother, wearing some outfit of indescribable beauty and design of many bright colors, stood in front of the people and commanded attention.

Give them something while they prepare to come out to prove that they are taking your daughter to a decent home," the lady whom I called the spokeswoman, informed the people. At this time I was lost in my expectations. "What kind of a marriage is this? couples are apart from each other . . .,?" I murmured to myself. All that I wanted to see was my wife but she was nowhere to be found. For some reason Mary did not alert me of anything. It was Teacher Amma who was doing the interpretation as much as she could. Mary was rather busy explaining to her coworkers who wanted to know more about the Ashanti marriage custom.

Within twenty minutes, all of us, I mean the foreigners who were strange to this culture, became astounded as an entourage of young, beautiful ladies appeared from one room. The spokeswoman, who was now wearing the Kente outfit, led them. Each of the ladies coming in a single file carried a load. At this instant more people rushed to the place. I had never seen that many people staring at me as today. To them I was like an actor in a Shakespearean play at the center stage but to me I was like Robinson Crusoe struggling in the Treasure Island but not knowing the extent of the treasure. Gee! They sang to herald the occasion. I wished I could understand the words that sounded so beautiful.

The people carrying the dowry items, stood in front of us in a semicircle behind the spokeswoman. Dora was shining like a star as she saw the beautiful items to be presented to her. The preparation, the pomp, the dignified people involved, the culture and the lyrics all added to the pageantry of the occasion. The drums and the music lifted my spirit into the heavens as the drums echoed and the women sang to the tune of the drums. To succeed to marry the woman I have strived so hard to woo was like enjoying a journey to the Paradise

"Agooo!!" said the spokeswoman, Nana Akoma, whose voice was like a mike.

"Ameeen!" said the cloud

"Where is teacher Amma?" she asked.

"Teacher Amma had just stepped out," someone said. The children went outside to look for her. I was surprised that Nana Akoma, who was first speaking some few English sentences changed to speak in their dialect when Teacher Amma (Bravasky Gunterville) arrived.

"I want you to explain to your country man everything I say so he will understand what he is giving to his wife and her family."

"Congratulations," Amma padded on my shoulder.

The woman kept talking to the family in their language and Amma promised to try her best to give detailed meaning of what was being said.

We are here this afternoon on behalf of Mr Jason, the son of Kwame Bonsu, who met the daughter of Papa Bonsu and MameYaa Manu in America. Owura (Mr.) Jason, wanted to come home so he wooed your daughter and won her beautiful heart. They have married in the white man's way. But Dora knows that she cannot forget her culture. She has brought her concubine (mpena), to marry her according to the dictates of her ancestors.

Owura Jason says he loves his wife and as you all know, overseas people can die for their lovers. Even though he was not born in the culture but he has learnt it overnight with the aid of her new family in Ghana. Owura Jason wants his wife to know that when he first met her she was wearing beautiful clothes, provided by her parents and now that Dora has become his wife, it would be his sole responsibility to put clothes on her beautiful body so that she would be excelled among all other Women, throughout their married lives.

There was a little period of silence. One of the females, who carrying about twelve different pieces of African fabrics of assorted colors, came forward. The people hummed. She slowly turned around 360 degrees for everyone to see what she was carrying. Nana Akoma continued her speech.

Mr. Jason gives his wife, Akosua Dora, these twelve pieces of cloths (six yards each). The load was placed in front of Dora. the people clapped. Two more ladies came forward, carrying more cloths. They turned around like the first one and Nana Akoma announced that five pieces of cloth (six yards each) to the mother, and three cloths (Twelve yards each) and twelve yards of Kente Cloth to his father-in-law. The cloud applauded for a long time. I could see Dora's father smiling for the first time since I came here.

We have not finished yet; Dora's husband is not from here. He is a gentleman and therefore he wants his wife to dress like any other lady when she is behind him. She gives to his wife seven designer dresses and two suits to match her African outfits. Again before Dora dresses up for the day, she would take showers; her husband gives her six sponges, pomade, powder, perfume, underwear, and bras. Mr. Jason gives to his wife four each of these items so that she will smell good, dress good the way he wants his wife-to look when she appears in public.

Teacher Amma did not want me to know what they said about it. The next person in line was a young beautiful lady, carrying sandals and shoes. When she came forward, she turned around and wow, she looked like a model. My wife knows me ... she turned around to look at me. I pretended to turn my gaze away from her. The beauty and the fashion of these Africans would make any foreigner look stupid for disrespecting them in their countries.

"We all know that Dora ye Awuraa (is a lady), when she dresses up she needs a nice pair of shoes to match. When she is dressed like the white person she will need shoes, when she dresses culturally she will need native sandals, therefore Mr. Jason gives to his wife five pairs of leather shoes, five pairs of native sandals. The goods were placed before Dora. Dora lifted up one of the sandals and smiled. It has some gold dust on it. The next person in line came forward.

Also Mr. Jason wants his wife to wipe her face if she needs to, also to show victory when it is needed and also to hold in her hand when doing cultural dances, therefore he gives to his wife, a hundred white handkerchiefs. The handkerchiefs were placed before her. I guess it was part of the culture. They gave some to the chief and the queen mother and within a twinkle of an eye the rest of the handkerchiefs were scrambled off by the crowd. Dora had to struggle to keep some of the handkerchiefs. Everyone was waving the white handkerchiefs in the air.

"Also Mr. Jason after getting his wife would like to enjoy what he is paying for so he wants his wife to dress the bed and the pillows so that he can be able to do his job properly in the night. By next year this time they will come back with little Dora or little Jason; he gives to his wife four bed sheets, and eight pairs of pillow cases and two bedspreads, beautifully crafted and hand sown. At this time I saw five guys standing at corner mumbling about something. I remembered about the plan of the brothers. I prayed that they would not be forgotten. I know two of them were Dora's brothers but the other three I didn't know.

Another lady, a middle-aged woman came forward with paper notes in a bowl. Apart from all the goods I have given my wife, an amount of $1,000 was given to my mother-in-law for taking care of Dora until I married her; an amount of $3,000 was also given to the father, $200 to the grandmother, fifty dollars each to her six aunts, and thirty dollars was dashed to each of her brothers and sisters. The brothers objected that the money was insufficient and if I did not increase they will not allow me to marry their sister. The family had to negotiate with them. Nobody explained the final decision to me.

"Mr. Jason has done well. Clap for him. Everyone clapped.

After Nana Akoma had finished the presentation, the linguist turned to the elders and the family and repeated everything that Nana Akoma had said. At this time the queen mother thanked us for what we have done but one more thing needed to be clarified before they accept those gifts.

"We cannot accept these gifts until we have heard from our daughter, grandchild or sister to tell us finally if she wants us to accept these," the linguist told my family.

This is the point they put a little drama into the episode. Mysteriously, Dora was missing from the crowd. They asking themselves where is Dora? Where is Dora? Nobody seemed to know where she was. As for this one they got me good. I was indecisive, could not figure out what was going on. No body, not even my family, hinted me about this. Her brothers came forward and announced that they knew where Dora was but it would take them some lorry fare (money for transportation) before they could bring her. I did not understand the significance of this stage of the culture. I did not know what happened, one of the brothers got angry and threatened that the marriage will not take place unless they get the money and she is their sister and they will never agree to the marriage if I could not fulfill their needs. This is the time I jumped in and got two fifty-dollar bills from my pocket and gave it to them. I could not believe their next move. They jumped for joy and bragged that they have found a good husband for their sister. Within a twinkle of an eye, Dora surfaced in the most beautiful outfit I have never seen on her. The women chanted making sounds like 'papabii! Papabi! This went on for a while around Dora. The melody was very sweet and I couldn't wait to find out what they were saying. I signaled to Teacher Amma and it was she who told me that papaabi the good one, the beautiful etc. I was satisfied with that about my wife. "What about me . . . no one is going to sing for me," I muttered within myself. Dora walked with six other ladies, all of them wearing the same style outfit except one of them who was wearing kente cloth. The girls were really beautiful especially one wearing the kente. It was planned in such a way that I could not see the face of Dora and many of the others. The girls were called one at a time to stand before me.

"Jason, is she the woman who is supposed to be your wife?" the linguist would ask me this question about each woman.

"No! This is not my wife, I need my Dora. I responded to each of them. But temptation fell on me on one of them, who happened to be Mercy. In retrospect, before Mercy came, Mary had given me a note.

"Be careful of what you say. If you accept any of them instead of Dora, you will be forced to marry her; this is part of the culture that the elders cannot deny your choice and all these dowries would go the woman of your choice. So be careful about Mercy." I slipped the note in my chest pocket. Immediately, Mercy was brought before me, wearing their elaborate traditional fabric called Kente. She was just like a model in Hollywood. Her beauty was beyond description but Dora's beauty from within was diamond and I did not hesitate to say no since everyone was quiet this time and staring at me.

"No where is my Dora," I rejected her right away.

The last one that came was my own Dora.

"Jason you spent a lot of money today on a beautiful flower in this town. Can you please tell us who is this girl?" I could not respond verbally and I moved forward and hugged her. Yes! Yes! Yes! Thank you all this is my wife. Everyone there clapped, drums were beaten, songs were sung by women and the children curiously looked on the faces of the adults. The scene was beautiful and I wished this culture will continue to abound.

"Komm! Komm (quiet! quite!)" the linguist shouted. I think it was a synonym of agoo! Everyone became quiet. It was teacher Amma who joined them to speak about my wife in English.

"Isn't she beautiful, look at her neck, the teeth, the bottom (she then tapped her butt)... you deserve this honor... you deserve to be in America to show your beauty... Oh Jason! You're the luckiest man."

When she finished, they clapped. I wondered what would follow next. "When are we to be declared as husband and wife? After all the dowries I have given them we are still yet to go through the cultural hurdles again." I wondered within

"Agooo!!!," shouted the linguist.

"Ameen!!!," the crowd responded. The place became silent again. Dora and the three other ladies faced Dora's father and the elders.

"Dora, a man called Jason, nobody knows him in this town... Do you know him? The father pointed to me.

"Yes Papa, I know him," responded Dora.

"He has come here today, and brought all these things for you so that you could be his wife. The family cannot answer him yes or no ...," There was a little moment of silence. Dora looked down and then gradually lifted up her golden countenance to have a glimpse of me. The father continued.

"Dora do you agree that I should accept these gifts?"

"Yes Papa, accept them," responded Dora.

"Dora, a man has come here and gave us all these items to me and the family. He wants you to be his wife. Do you agree that I should accept these gifts? Give me your final answer for everyone to witness so that in future you will not come to me with any complains about your husband. The people here are my witnesses."

"Yes Papa, accept them ...," responded Dora the second time. "But papa, pray for me that he will continue to be a good husband."

"Yes Papa, accept them...." The women kept fanning Dora as if she was the queen mother with big and wild beautiful straw fans.

The last thing to be done to pave way for the traditional marriage, was for Dora to come and choose from among the crowd her husband to be. She held a glass of wine in her hand and she combed through the crowd to identify the husband to be. That was the happiest part of the whole occasion. Dora moved from man to man in her attempt to identify me. All the men were calling her to come to choose them. Finally she came to me and hugged me and gave me a sip of the wine. I got it from her and likewise gave her a sip also. We walked and stood in front of the people. The crowd applauded and gave us a standing ovation.

"What did I do to earn this honor ... ?" I murmured to myself. Dora held onto my hand and walked me to the middle. The spokeswoman came to us with a copper plate. She picked up a gold ring and gave it to Dora to put on my hand.

"Ashanti is a land of gold. That's why the white man called this place the 'Gold Coast' and we do not want you to go back without a piece of gold on you," said the lady. After that Dora put the ring on my hand. Wow! It was big and heavy. She also gave Dora's ring to me to put on her fingers. Having done that we hugged and all the sisters, five altogether, came and hugged me.

There was brief pomp, dancing and everyone waved their white handkerchiefs. Now I saw the significance of giving out the handkerchiefs. They shook our hands and spoke their dialect to me as if I understood.

Instantly, I wanted to kiss Dora and tossed her around in my arms but her culture debars me from doing that. I could do none of these because of the culture- no kissing in the public. The linguist called for silence. By this time many of the people had left except the immediate family members. The chief spoke through the linguist to bless our union with some advice.

"Men spend a lot of money for a wife, but their main responsibility to a wife is to take care of the financial needs. Her children, properties and wealth would not be for you. Your responsibility is to make babies out of her to multiply her maternal family. Remember again and again that your wife comes from a matrilineal society and you and your family has no control over her and her children. Whenever the marriage is over, for some reason, Dora and her children belong here. No Ashanti blood goes anywhere and denounces his or her origin. I hope you understand that. We are a proud nation and people."

"I see . . . ," I nodded in agreement.

It was at this instant I realized that I was marrying the entire family and not Dora alone. After the ceremony was over, they asked the family members to be seated. I sat on the right side of my father, the man who generously spent his money to see that I got to marry Dora according to the dictates of their custom. My mother was sitting on the left followed by Mary and her friends. The entire Dora's relatives got up, led by Mame Amma Dufie and followed by Dora . . . came and shook our hands one at a time. This time I learnt a new vocabulary. Everyone who shook my hand said, "wo yere da w'ase" which was later interpreted as "your wife thanks you." I realized that Dora and her sisters were the only ones who hugged me. Ever since I arrived, even though I was struggling to marry Dora, the sisters treated me like their own husbands.

Now I realized the significance of what I did for Dora when I offended her during our dating period. Had it not been for the love of Mr. Mensa and Madam

Addae, I would have missed this girl without the slightest understanding as why she behaved the way she carried herself from the beginning. The beauty of it all was the culture, which we had been made to understand as primitive. This is the time I had wanted to visit Mr. Mensa who, I understand, was deported to Ghana before we left. Dora insisted that she would not let me see him because he might still be bitter about what happened to him. I hated her conclusion.

"I have nothing to do with that ... those white folks ... ," Afro-Americans tend to treat us worse than the whites. It's true but the majority of us do not understand." I gave up the argument because I am not too good in debating with my wife. I realized some truth in what she was saying and how they were treated at my party. But now I have come to know that Africans and Afro-Americans are the same; the differences are the cultural bridges separating us. I asked Mary why Dora's sisters treated me like their husbands.

... your sister-in-laws are considered to be your wives and will treat you just like their own husbands in the absence of your wife with an exception that it is a taboo to sleep with them."

This was really a moral education for me for all the filthy thoughts in me over the years was being cleansed away from me. At that instance I recollected the immoral behavior, just as what has been mentioned to me, of a friend of mine who was dating look alike twin sisters at the same period. One of them was his girlfriend who did not know that he was also dating her younger twin sister. One day the motel desk clerk became curious about the girls and started asking questions. He told him the truth that they were twins. Such thoughts rummaged through my mind including many cases of incest. So this new vocabulary of taboo was so religiously inspiring and changed me from thinking immorality to that of morality with only Dora in the center stage. Mary realized that I became very thoughtful of her statement.

"I work at your embassy so I hear such embarrassing stories everyday. Just don't bring that over here," she padded me on the back

"What's going on with you guys?" Dora, who was anxious to know what we were talking about interrogated.

Chapter Ten

It felt so good inside me, having satisfied all the traditional requirements. It was like a dream come true for the impossibility to be possible.

"Now it's all over . . . we can now do anything in our own married world. No more parental control. Wow it's like buying a wife," I became crazy with joy over my achievement. My happiness was halted for a while when Mary hinted me that the people had not finished with me yet. I did not like the idea but I had no other choice. Dora and I were given seats next to each other.

The elders started speaking in their dialect one after the other. Sister Mary and Teacher Amma took pains to make sure I understood everything they said. The following is a summation of the advice provided by the elders:

In Ashanti we call marriage aware (a long journey); a journey destined to end only by death. It is a union between families, individuals, tribes, nations, and at the same time it can create wars and scuffles of all kinds. Therefore it would be proper for those who wanted to be united in marriage to understand the responsibilities involved. Marriage is a symbol of a broom, the handle is the man (Almighty) the breadwinner and therefore if a man is ready to take a wife he should be ready to feed the wife and the children that would be born. The sticks or the straws represent the two families bounded equally together because of this marriage, and the ribbon or the rope is what bounds you two together.

Another elder continued. In Ashanti the children belong to the mother; they inherit their brothers, sisters, uncles, nephews etc.

In your country--I understand–are of patrilineal system based on the Western culture. You have to realize that you have no full control over your wife. You are just her caretaker for the benefit of her family. If she encountered some problems or finds herself in debt, then it would be your responsibility as a husband to save her from disgrace.

Another elderly lady intervened: Dora, you have a great responsibility to your husband. He spent his money, time, and effort to endure this pain to marry you. From now on you must realize that in Ashanti, men are not familiar with the kitchen. Therefore, it's your obligation, as a wife, to feed your husband until the end of the journey. A woman does not complain of hunger to a man because a man has no business in the kitchen. In the same token a man does not approach a woman for chop money because a man is to till the soil to make money for the family. Men are obligated to go to war, cut the bushes for farms and hunt for meat. Men plant the cash crops and the women grow the grocery products in the farms. Men make the babies and women carry and nurture them.

Mame Amma Dufie joined: Be aware that Dora is a princess in this town and be careful that your children would have no trouble with the law. In this tribe a prisoner, a thief, or one involved with the drugs trade, are all prevented to hold any position of authority or inherit any chieftaincy throne.

I hope you understand this carefully.

You are now free to have your wife and you are expected to make babies and that's all we want from you. We have the right to end this marriage if after two or three years you are not able to prove your manhood."

Wow, it was very instructional and I loved it. The part I did not understand was me taking care of her financially and the ownership of the children. There was no cause of argument because when we go back to the States, the financial obligation stuff and the children would not apply.

"Now the ceremony is completed and now Akosua Dora and . . . ," the speaker paused when he was about to mention my name. He did not want to call me Mr. Jason. He turned to Dora.

"What's your husband's name?" Dora looked at me.

"They know my name"

Mary and her father came and surrounded me.

"On what day were you born?"

"I don't know . . . September 20, 1956."

This was the time I became very embarrassed. It was very strange to the people that did not know the day I was born. Until now, I didn't know it was that important. I did not even know if my parents will remember the day my brothers and sisters were born without the aid of the calendar. We don't keep such records . . . the Government keep them. Luckily Mary had a calendar on her.

"He was born on a Saturday." Everyone clapped.

"Akwaaba . . . Kwame . . . Akwaaba . . . Kwame." This is the first time I did not need any interpretation.

"Well we have come to a conclusion; Akosua and Kwame are now husband and wife. Your Akan name is Jason Kwame Bonsu. And you can use Jason as middle initial."

"I like that . . . it's a nice name," I agreed to your suggestion.

"Your children would be Bonsu not Washington."

After everyone else had spoken, the queen mother concluded the advice by conversing with us in English because, according to her, she wanted me to have a clear understanding of what was going on. She gave a brief history of the two families. She said with pride that despite the size of the village, it was older than many cities in the world. She made me to realize that Dora's extended family is large, over five hundred members, all scattered around the country and abroad.

"Due to the extended family system, the elders are very keen in monitoring marriages to avoid incest."

"Nana, thank you for your advice in English . . . ." said Dora.

"I have to let go tradition sometimes, so that your husband can understand all these cultural lessons he is taking."

"Nana, you are right, it's more than a classroom work-its pragmatic, visionary and feeling of it transforms natural beauty," I said. She shook my hand and blessed us to go for the Almighty would be with us always.

Everyone had spoken and I had to do my part. Mary had to instruct me as what to do and say."Say, "Mate ne nyinaa, me ne me yere da mo ase pii." (I have heard everything that was said and my wife and I thank you) said Mary and I had to repeat after her in their language. I was shaking hands with everyone saying mate ne nyinaa, me ne me yere da mo ase pii. Teacher Amma joined us when she entered and could speak the language very fluently.

They clapped their hands for us and there was a little fanfare of dancing with their highlife music. Dora held my hand and started dancing around me. All her sisters joined and hit my head with white handkerchiefs. The joy was extended to the whole curious community.

They walked us outside; Dora and I waved to anybody who passed by.

Out of the ordinary, a medium aged woman with a baby tied on her back confronted us and started a quarrel with Dora. I became so confused about the behavior of this woman. I hate it when someone wants to mess up with my woman. I have been in many fights because of situations like this.

"What does the culture expect me to do?" I murmured to myself.

"Why do you bring over here all these troubles and confusion...?" said the lady who spoke in English.

"Leave me alone," replied Dora. "What is this...are you crazy? I assumed the people understood where the woman was coming from because they just stood around to watch them talk.

"Yes I am crazy... because you are the queen mother's daughter...,"

"Let's go inside," my father intervened my anger and walked me inside.

"Father, why? That woman might beat Dora," "Let her beat her. You have nothing to do with women fighting. In this community, because of the practice of poligamy, men never separate two women from fighting. If you do that the woman would charge that you helped your wife to beat her."

"Now I do understand."

"You can only watch them." We went to the front door but their scuffle was over and Dora was very angry and raining insults at the woman.

"You all can fuss all you want, the game is over and Dora is now my wife," I murmured

It was teacher Amma, who knew everything that occurred in the community, who told me the woman was angry because her family prevented her from marrying a stranger from Nigeria. She loved the man but they would not even let the man bring the kokooko. She was angry because Dora was allowed to get married to me.

"Wow! I think this people eat, sleep and dance with culture. This is a different world, a new history book...," I marveled.

"Whatever it is, you have your wife and make sure when you go home you won't let this be a waste with your own doing," she said.

Everything is now over. We walked under an orange tree behind the house and all the oranges on the tree were ripened with a lot of rotten oranges lying on the ground. I stretched my hand and plucked an orange fruit from its branch.

"If you want an orange, the children can get some for you," said Dora.

"Do you know this is my first time of coming closer to an orange tree and even to the extent of plucking an orange from its branch?"

"Oh I forget you are from the winterland, snow everywhere, dead leaves everywhere and allergy flying around like these birds over here," commented Dora. I really did not get it, why she said that but there was truth in what she said.

Chapter Eleven

After the function, the people dispersed to their various homes. My family also asked for permission to leave, to return to Kumasi. My father asked that Dora and I should spend our first night with them but Dora's family strongly disagreed to that suggestion. They debated this peacefully and Dora's family won so we had to spend our first night as husband and wife with Dora's family.

Before my parents left, they advised me to come to Kumasi within three days. I had no choice and like Dora, I have to concur with my parents' wishes. The whole community became concerned when my people were leaving. It was another memorable occasion to witness how the people show love and excitement to see loved ones going away from the village. I leaned on a mango tree and marveled. To my surprise mango fruits started falling on me and everywhere around me. The people struggled to pick them up and started sucking the juice from the oval-shaped fruits. My daddy beckoned to me to come closer to him. "Be aware, the falling of the mango signifies fruitfulness in the womb," my father whispered. I laughed and he tapped me on the back. The people are so spiritually collected together that they have an explanation to every incident. I guess this is what the white man called superstition. I think one has to understand the whole cultural atmosphere of a people before calving a name for their beliefs. Dora picked up a big rounded mango fruit. After washing it, she tenderly squeezed all around it and it became as soft as her tidies. She bit the top and put it in my mouth to suck the juice. I had tried the mango fruit a couple of times since I had been here and I liked it very much. I just pondered over what my father had just told me. I wanted that to happen more than anything else. While I was sucking the juice out of the mango, all my eyes were concentrated on her breast. How I wished, I was home and in my room alone with her.

"The Mango juice is sweet but you are sweeter. Let's get out of here and go somewhere," I whispered in her ear. The people were irritated when Dora put the mango in my mouth. They started grumbling and I heard some words sounding like oburoni. Aburokyirefo-Already I knew the meaning of Oburoni (white man) and I learned later that aburokyirefo means 'overseas people or white people.' The words I whispered in her ears had occupied her mind because she knew exactly what I meant. But it was impossible for us to show any romantic moods in that closed cultured community. "Who cares much about someone going out of town?" I murmured with awe. This was the time that I wished I could understand their dialect. I loved to witness them hugging and smiling among themselves when they gather together.

The driver, who was waiting to drive my family to the city, became impatient, I presumed. He blew the horn continuously and the passengers responded with a rush. It worked; within minutes, everyone rushed to board the vehicle while the people were crowding around the car. It was at this time that Dora and I shook my parent's hands to express our appreciation and gratitude for the part they played in our marriage.

"Americans thank you all," I said while kissing my palm and waving it toward them.

My daddy looked up and down and retorted,

"Only the heavens know what happened to our people in your country. We hope that Nana Nyame (God) would bring all of them back here, one at a time, You have come home to unite with us," said my father. Another elder, contributed with his broken heavy accent; "My children, Sankofa is not a taboo but rather a blessing." The way he said that was so funny that everyone laughed. But to me I was contemplating on the new vocabulary 'sankofa' but I could not ask any questions at that time. At this time my mother alighted from the front of the car, and gave us a warm hug.

"It is God who did everything according to His wishes and we will see you all soon in Kumasi," she said and then boarded the car again.

Everyone waved 'bye' while the vehicle was disappearing from the village and others were saying something like nante yie!, nante yie! Moments later, they disappeared from the scene. I felt like kissing my wife in appreciation for the part she played toward our constitutional and traditional unions, but I wasn't bold enough to create any ethical confusion. Instead, I hugged her very tightly and whispered in her ears: "I love you and will continue to cherish you, with all my heart, muscles and bones, only death will make us depart." She loosened herself from me and then replied with a hug again. The whole community watched us hugging each other with mixed feelings and silent comments that could easily be detected from their countenances. They behaved like they were watching a movie from a theater screen. "We will see . . . its time for you to be a man," she said.

We held our hands and sneaked into the house. It was at this time I presumed that we were going on some kind of a honeymoon. When I mentioned it to my wife, she just laughed. She pointed to a corner. I could not believe what I saw-- prepared meals of assorted tastes were lined up.

"Why?" I asked.

"You have not seen anything yet."

"Wonderful Ashanti," I said. She told them that I had to change my clothes before we eat. When I entered the chamber to change, she quickly came in and started fondling with my body.

"Me first," she said. To me the heavens poured down stimulating surprises. She threw me on the bed and took her time to undress me and telling my balls to get ready for her. The most sexiest moment was the time she took to naked her silky black complexioned body in an ocean of smiles, watching me lying down and reaching the peak of my arousal. She threw her flexible body on me and immediately we wasted no time in mixing the hot and the cold waters within us aiming to catch a fish, a fish that would be a blessed conclusion of what we had just gone through.

"This is going to be our honeymoon, the African way," said Dora. My wife is bad and could be thirsty for sex sometimes but at times she would behave that she hated sex. It was like heaven had fallen down on me when I was waking up her rose buds (tidies) my favorite love play. For twenty minutes we really caressed each other with one aim in mind-making love. I mean making love to a woman you have suffered so hard to win makes you feel like a real man. Truly I was a real man with a new name: Jason Kwame Bonsu.

"I love you; I love you," she kept on saying, while I was turning her on by doing my own thing.

"Me... too, honey," I said, while giving her a cozy kiss and with my arms caressing all over her chocolate body.

"I love you too...," she said in a soft sweet tone. "Give me my baby now."

Now I could feel the softness of the whole body as if all the bones in her body had been transformed into a fresh new baby.

"Give me my baby now," she repeated.

My wife's statement struck me. I remembered what my father whispered to me concerning the falling mango fruits.

"Today is my day," I said.

"I don't blame you for what I have put you through," she responded. Compared to my formal woman who had only a great sexual passion but Dora has everything good associated with womanhood: the body, the shape, manners and cultural orientation which made her unique and special among women.

She became so passionately crazy that she bit me without knowing. Before I could comment on anything, someone knocked on the door. She wanted to get up right away but I held her down to finish what I was doing. The person behind the door kept calling

"Sister, Sister..."

"Wait, I am coming," she replied while she was putting on her clothes.

"Who is that?" asked Dora

"It's me Stella," she said. "Maame sent me to give you a bowl of water," she continued and handed the bowl to Dora and then left. Later, having relaxed my nerves, I joined her in the living room. We ate, we conversed-- almost about everything--and laughed over certain things especially the lack of privacy in Africa. But for some reason I began to think about my family back home.

"I wish... I am sorry," I said suddenly, interrupting her.

"That's one thing that I don't like about you. You have the tendency of changing your trend of thoughts anytime." The children came over and carried away the plates. We went to the bedroom where she wanted to know more about my absent-minded behavior.

"What's on your mind?" she asked.

"Anything... I was just thinking about my people—I don't even know what to call my people now–when are we going to enjoy your beautiful cultural environment?

"There you go again . . . changing the topic," she said.

"I wish my sister will remain single until I go back home. I will make sure nobody comes to our house and take any of my sisters for granted anymore. Her suitors have to experience what I had to go through with you."

"You think it's that easy. It's the culture that compares people to do these things. You don't have this traditional culture but rather a constitutional setup. I am sorry about that but that is the truth. Even though what she said has some truth to it but I insisted that culture or no culture I will introduce it to my people, else I would advise Darlene to marry an African. She laughed and I became offended about her ironic mood. I took a few steps away from her.

"Don't be offended. I am just speaking my mind-the truth. You have to accept something before you can modify or change it."

"I do understand you now. You're just a wise woman, I am glad I married you," I said.

"This is what we call Sankofa in our dialect," said Dora

"I have been hearing about this word Sankofa from several sources. What does that mean? It sounds so sweet like Swahili,"

"Your people and the Swahili culture. I don't think there is any Swahili blood among your ancestors," she said.

"So when you are in Ashanti, the core of African slavery, don't worry about any other tribe. This is your true home."

"I don't know; we are still learning from each other. I wasn't sure I would be allowed to marry you and now that we are married we have to meet each other's culture halfway."

"I understand perfectly well that our love and any other love between the African and the Africans in the Diaspora will be described as Sankofa

"What is Sankofa?"

"It's a proverb our elders gave us-a sign of a bird that has turned its neck and looking behind. It literally means whatever you left behind, don't be ashamed to go back for it."

"What has that got to do with me and my sister?"

"Just like what you are doing now, going back to your roots in Africa despite what others think and never to be ashamed of it."

"I see; so you think my sister won't marry an African for him to do the same thing to my sister?"

"The same thing like what?"

"I mean the dowries-for each member of my family, the kokooko and all the other cultural stuff," I said

"Well if you put something where it doesn't belong, it will fail eventually. You cannot inherit a culture overnight," she answered with an African proverb.

"Perhaps you may educate your family for them to adopt the African culture and practice it."

"You are frank and communicative to me nowadays. I never knew we could be like this today. Ever since we have been together we have never conversed like this long. Now I know who I married.

"I know because before the traditional marriage I regarded you as *mpena* (a friend) not a husband. The title of a husband is not easily achieved."

"I see so you were planning to desert me if your people did not agree?"

"What would I have done. You don't understand, nobody in this culture would ever defy the wishes of parents. That happens in your country. I am sorry, now you have me you can do anything you want . . . eat me up," she said jovially.

"I just pray that nothing again would come between us again. I will do my best to educate my people."

"You have a big task to do then." We conversed until we fall asleep without even giving each other a goodnight kiss. I had a miscalculated dream. I saw Yolanda fussing with my mother. I know that girl, when she is angry about something she would resonate whatever she says.

"I learned that your son is in the African jungles so that they can do some marriage rituals on him after making me pregnant. He thinks he is going to marry an African jungle lady instead of me? As soon as they return, we will see," said Yolanda. My mother leaned back . . . and held a branch from a tree.

"Yolanda, what are you talking about? I understand you and Jason broke up more than six months ago. How can you be pregnant with him?" said my mother while letting the branch to go off from her grip.

"You want to know what your son can do? You better advise him not to come here with any ass holed African woman and we will see who belongs to this country. These foreigners come to this country to take our everything."

"Jason is a grown up man and he can do anything without my permission. You must realize that Jason is my son... and you have the nerves to disrespect?" said my mother.

"You can do whatever you want to do because you can't force yourself on my son." The dream then shifted to a different scene where Yolanda and I were having a drive-through type of romance extravaganza in my blue car. In the dream I was holding her tight in the car and to my surprise Dora shook me and I awoke from my sleep. I found myself back in Africa lying next to my soft and flexible Dora. I rushed to use the rest room. I contemplated on what that dream might mean and I wished Yolanda won't do anything harmful to any of us when we return to the States. As for the pregnancy it was a fabrication. Whatever it might be I was convinced that my new culture (Sankofa) will not make it possible to lose my wife under any circumstances. I could not sleep again until early in the morning. That was the night I had wanted to sleep until late in the morning and have my morning loving exercise with her. This loving exercise which I created helps couples to arouse their sexuality for the enjoyment of both partners. Since I have been in Africa we have not got chance to do it. But my plan did not work out because of this cultural stuff.

According to my wife's assertion, wives must get up early in the morning to wash before they can talk to anybody. They feel shy and unclean for everyone to assume that they had sex with their husbands. To me it was one of the craziest things I have heard. "Who cares whether somebody had sex or not?" I murmured to myself. I had to force it to have some loving before the cock crew.

"I have to go and take my bath before everybody gets up," she said immediately the cock crew.

"What do you mean? We have not finished yet."

She looked at me and shook her head before kissing me.

"This is Africa you know. It's a communal association not an individualism," she said and then rushed out the door. To her surprise, one of her sisters, had already brought us a bucket full of warm water to bathe. Dora bathed first. When she finished, I was expressing my displeasure of taking baths in her country. They had no hot water faucets, I had to bathe with boiled water from a bucket. Suddenly someone came to the door.

"I think my sister is calling you...," said Dora.

I went to the door to meet the sister. She smiled at me without saying anything.

"Good morning. . . ." I said. She responded with a smile and then informed me that my water was ready in the bathroom. I was provided with everything I needed for bathing-soap, towel, sponge and rubber slippers. It took me about fifteen minutes to finish bathing from a bucket of luke-warm water. That was a great experience of bathing from a bucket. It was like going through a ritual but I had to do that ever since I have been here.

"What took you so long? Dora asked when I came back. I didn't answer her because one of her sisters was in the room.

"There is one more thing for us to do in order to conclude our marriage."

"What again . . . ," I murmured to myself. We did not even finish eating when we were called to come down. Unbelievably, the yard was crowded with the neighbors. It was like everyone in the neighborhood had entered the house. As usual we decided to stand up and all the scores of the people came to us and shook our hands. My wife explained that they had just come to congratulate us because for completing our marriage rituals and some of them were just being nosy to see the man Dora married.

Wearing my green Dashiki, I blended in with the people, and it could hardly be detected that I was a stranger among them. Everything went on smoothly well during our first day of marriage. Everyone seemed to be happy with the union; I could see it on Dora's face with a thousand of smiles and exposing her beautiful dimples all the time.

During the third day at Boma a vehicle arrived from Kumasi about noon and my parents sent a message that I should come to Kumasi in that particular vehicle.

"We are adults and why can't these people leave us alone. Now he is controlling me like I am a baby," I muttered. I guess Dora was contemplating the same thoughts. She grasped my hand.

"Let's go," she said. For a while Kumi and I have not been having fun together so I was delighted to have him in our company. She took me to almost every home just to say goodbye to them before I left. Most of the people did not speak English so the language echoed in my ears like the sounds of a mockingbird singing in the backyard. The palace (Ahenfie) where the chief resides was the last place we visited. Just before we entered the palace, someone told Dora's family that she was taking me to visit the chief. The family joined us. They instructed me on how to do things in the palace. It was the biggest house in the town and seemed to be the center of everything in the village.

"Is Nana home?" asked Dora.

"*Awuraba* (lady), yes. You can come in." a young guy wearing a piece of cloth around his waist led us in. It was the most memorable occasion in my life. I have been seeing African drums but the drums that I saw in the palace were amazing. Two of the drums were bigger and taller than me. The rest consisted of various shapes and designs. Suddenly, the drummers commenced beating the drums. I was lost in my imagination. Now I know Africa is the origin of black music and instruments. These drums, the big ones could be heard about a mile away. The people came in from the surrounding houses to contribute to the dancing and the merriment. I had to dance in my own way with Dora and the crowd surrounded, called us by some names in their dialect and poured white powder all over us. After the fanfare, we have to appear before the chief and his elders.

We lined up in a queue led by the oldest sister. We greeted the chief and his elders. This time I had no problem with the greeting ethic. I removed my shoes accordingly and bowed while shaking the chief's hands. He said something in Twi but nobody interpreted it to me. As soon we finished the greetings, the drummers started drumming for about ten minutes.

"My children . . ." the chief addressed us through the linguist. "May the gods and our ancestors bless your marriage with many children."

The crowd responded with some uu! sound which I cannot describe, followed with laughter

Awuraa, (lady) you brought a man to his ancestral home to marry you but this is what our ancestors preached against. We are encouraged not to marry strangers. That's why they told us a folk tale story about that beautiful young girl, Oforiwaa, who disobeyed her parents' choice for her and ended up marrying a crocodile. I hope you know that *Ananse* (spider) story. But since *Nana Hemaa* (Queen mother) gave you her blessing, you may then be allowed to marry the stranger. Remember in the past, people have married strangers who were: diseased, ghosts, impotent, thieves. But due to the circumstances surrounding your husband, we give you our blessing, peace and love but if you go to his home and find anything negative remember that you belong here. According to our culture, you and your children will never belong to him because we are matrilineal. I hope he understands that."

The people applauded after the chief's advice and then the drummers started drumming again. While the drumming was going on, the people left the palace one after the other. Before we left, I counted about twenty different kinds of drums. I wanted to interview the drummers but there was not enough time.

Dora told her people something in Twi and soon after that they left our presence.

"We have to go and thank the queen mother also," she said.

"I can't wait to see her. She really made it possible for our union."

"What else do you expect? She is in charge of all the women in the town."

I was skeptical to see her since she had power to cause anything to happen. At the same time I was anxious to know what kind of advice she was also going to give.

The people that were in the queen mother's palace were mostly men including the linguist. The linguist asked us to wait in the veranda, while the Queen mother was getting ready. Dora took the opportunity to enlighten me about some of the things I did not understand.

"I hope you know that I am a member of the royal family; this queen mother, Nana Oforiwaa is a part of my family, my mother's older sister."

"You're just joking."

"That's why she did not enforce the traditional rules." Ten minutes later she emerged from her room in a gorgeous outfit, followed by three ladies and three men. What marveled me about her was the decoration of gold jewelry on her. Her headband was a thick gold ring. When she sat down she asked those around her to leave her presence.

"I am glad that you have married my daughter. You could not have married her without my signature," she spoke in English. "You must take good care of her because when I die she may be the one to take my place. One of your children may be the chief of this town one day so make sure you raise them well. My heart was full of joy and I kept smiling. I felt so happy for my wife and unborn children to be in such a glorious position.

"Really?" I asked with excitement.

"Why do you ask. What do you think I am?" Dora intervened.

"You are delighted but your children may not be able to inherit the stool. Your children would be royals but they would need to speak the language before they could inherit anything," she looked at Dora whose countenance showed some sadness. This cultural thing can eat deep into your bones.

"That's why the elders were trying to prevent the marriage because of the future. In this culture we look before we marry."

"Nana, I promise all my children would be taught to speak Twi. They would be raised in the culture before coming to the states for their higher education." Nana was happy with my statement. She stretched her hand and we shook. "Me daase (I thank you).

"Your wife is aware of the consequences of loving you but she chose this cause. She knows that no non-Twi speaking person can inherit any proper stool in this culture; so beware." When the queen concluded her advice, Dora bowed and thanked her. Momentarily, tears came from her eyes. At this point she called the interpreter to talk to us, if he had anything more to add. The man also took the opportunity to address me in his own authority.

"My son," he turned to me. "You are lucky. In the past, no stranger came here with this kind of your mission. Nobody from this family marries a stranger but I don't know what you did to make her to fall in love with you. It's very unusual. The ancestors might have given her to you but remember she is not a chicken to be caught and slaughtered or forced to do anything against her will. Treat her like a human being. Remember, whatever she becomes in the future will be to the glory of her family at Boma."

He continued talking until the Queen intervened and asked him to make his point. My wife was just sobbing. I became a little scared....My faith rested on my adopted father. I began to think about my father's request for me to return to Kumasi.

"Love is blind, and I didn't think about all these implications. My sisters were trying to tell me but I never listened."

"You may go now," said the queen mother. She asked Dora to come back later to see her because there was something wrong with her stomach.

"The die is cast and we just have to pray to the ancestors for one of them to come back to the world through my womb." These words were a great encouragement to my soul. This is the period I realized that Dora was truly on my side. I turned around and embraced her. Before we turned loosed,

Kumi was standing behind us. He had come to call me because the driver was ready to leave.

"I think I am pregnant," she whispered in my ears."

"Don't be crazy. You just had your period five weeks ago."

"The queen mother and the old ladies are very good in detecting pregnancies. We can't hide anything from the old ladies."

"How do you prove this?"

"When she said 'come on and see me tonight . . . there is something wrong with your stomach' that's what she was implying"

"I have no more comments. You're too much."

"I will see you soon in the city," she said while we were about to enter her house. We wished each other the final goodbye and I boarded the vehicle to go to Kumasi.

Chapter Twelve

I had mapped out what to do or see with my wife before leaving the country. The first sightseeing with Seth was so interesting that I thought of having another one when Dora comes to join me.

In Kumasi I was received with joy but I could sense that there was some kind of disagreement between my mother and father.

In the evening I went and sat by mother near the fireplace. She lifted her right arm and laid it on my shoulders.

"My son, what can I do for you now?" Everything is over now and I hope you are happy."

"Mom I don't know how to express my inner joy about the demonstration of your beautiful culture before me," I said.

"That's nice of you. But how come some of you people when you come over here and take pictures of our culture you make it look that we are stupid people," questioned my mother. I became very sad and guilty about her statement and I did not want our conversation to continue in that direction. What my mother said was printed in all our geography and history books. I just had to change the direction of our conversation.

"I thank you for all that you have done for me. You have shown me that you are a true mother and you will always be in my heart." Today I had to confess to her about my ignorance about them before I came to Africa. I was so naive about the place that I thought I was coming to the jungles to sleep in a hut around wild animals. I asked for forgiveness because I did not know. When I said that Mame Selina (she prefers me to call her by that) looked at me so hard without altering a word. After a while tears were drooping down her cheeks. I became embarrassed and could not know what to do.

"Mother what's wrong . . . ?" I asked. I went to call my father.

"This son here was totally lost. He thinks Ashantis sleep with animals. Why didn't Amma Dora teach him more about the Ashantis?" Mame Selina explained to Papa Bonsu.

"Why do you have to cry for this? He is now here with us and his eyes are opened. He will go back and bring his people to taste the sweetness of the motherland, a land of the slaves and a land of the originality of life and civilization." My father turned to me and warned me to be careful when I am talking to women because behind their eyelids is nothing but water.

"Ashantis believe that they are the wisest people on earth so don't say anything to degrade them," warned my father. I felt so ashamed that I had to move away from them to be by myself.

Today I am proud to be part of the African culture which is rooted in the history of my people. I have learnt so much since I arrived but I cannot mention them all now because my problem alone could go on forever if I were to give all the details of my marriage adventures and the related stories. Now I have the wife I needed, even though I have been well informed that she doesn't belong to me and I have no total control over her. Now that I am part of the culture I should not bother about anything for my children would belong here and enjoy their ancestral heritage. I was waiting for Dora to come from Boma so that we can enjoy our married life. On Saturday we got a message that Dora would come to conclude our marriage ceremony on Sunday. During the night I spent most hours to arrange my room to be cozy for her when she comes back. I asked my family what I had to do. They just replied "nothing." I woke up early in the morning on Sunday and got myself ready to wait for Dora and her people. I looked at myself in the mirror and admired myself with the black pants and a designer white shirt on me. "You look good," I told myself. The time is about eleven O'clock nothing was happening nor have I been served with Breakfast. I was getting hungry but I could not ask for food. Mary entered my room and informed me that I didn't have to eat anything until I saw my wife. I was too hungry to talk to her.

The drama started around noon. A nice looking lady, wearing a white cloth, entered and followed by several women. They talked for a while in their dialect and then my father commanded them to do something. Next, followed my wife, wearing a gorgeous white African attire with a white powder poured all over her body. I was directed to stand between my parents. Behind Dora was a single file of young women and girls, all carrying something that were covered with white towels. They rested their loads in the middle of the open-yard in a nice circle. "What might these be beneath the towels?" I wondered. The spokeswoman informed the gathering that Akosua Dora was now about to be joined fully to her husband Jason Kwame Bonsu. A woman's place is in the kitchen. To prove that she can feed her husband during the course of their marriage, she has presented this aduane kese (big feast) for her husband and his entire family." Her speech was responded to with a certain prolonged sound I cannot explain.

This is one of the disappointing moments to me since I have been here. I wondered why Dora would spend money for such a big feast instead of using the money to buy something to last. The culture would not even let them detect my feelings. The whole community was joyous and some people were carrying bowls and plates. In the midst of all that Dora walked over to me and poured powder all over me, a sign to reveal her husband to the world. I got up and hugged her–how I wished we had kissed each other.

The spokeswoman walked me to each dish and explained to me what they were and some of the ingredients used to prepare them. Most of the foods presented, were familiar: the fufu; the peanut butter soup (nkatekwan); the melon seeds soup (egusi); the palm soup (abe nkwan), the okro soup (nkruma nkwan); the famous spinach (nkontomire) stew; the corned beef stew decorated with whole boiled eggs; the plantain, the boiled green plantain, Abetee (casava fufu) with okra soup and a big bowl of rice and many others including fresh fruits.

There was not much culture associated with this, just a wife cooking for the husband the first time after marriage. The people just got some food to take home. I just stood there with my arms folded to watch the display of the people, a culture that bonds people, community and nations together through marriage. "No matter they don't honor our type of marriage," I murmured.

"Now I understand well that I married the entire family and the community at large," The meals for the family were separately kept.

The males sat around a big dining table after those who do not live in the house had left. My wife did not go but remained in my room while the men were eating. This was an excruciating experience to me; eating together with many people from the same bowl especially without the aid of the fork or knife was something that was beyond my comprehension. I forced myself to adapt so quickly for the sake of the woman I loved.

Finally I had Dora to myself without any parental controls. Already my father has assured me that once I have done everything, Dora could not make any attempt to divorce me as long as he lived. With less than a week for us to return home, I had my lasting moments with her during the night with the hope of coming back to Ghana again with our own baby.

The first on our agenda was to go for sight seeing through the city. Unlike Kumi, she chose the places she wanted us to visit. We had more time to be by ourselves as we didn't have to worry about any more cultural restrictions. What I had to do now was to comport myself and behave like a decent husband as we tour the city. There were so many slim ladies walking around in their multicolored clothes which I had to manage to sneak to look at them. It was her habit, when we were in the states, to scold me for looking at other women. First we went to the Kumasi Central Market, the place I avoided to go with Kumi. The open market is like five or six shopping malls conglomerated together like a metamorphous rock. It was the largest and the most congested place I had ever been. Every trading activity took place in this place, except that there was no police nor security personnel present.

Interacting with the traders was an experience I will never forget. It was the first time I really experienced human congestion rather than traffic. Every aspect of the market was congested. The traders, mostly women, were squeezed in their little congested shelves where they have stored everything they had to sell. The shelves or stores are laid out in long rectangular grids. The major sections were named according the products sold in these shelves. We spent a lot of time at the jewelry and fabric sections.

The aisle is so narrow that people just had to run into each other. The people are used to touching each other. They don't even care when someone steps on their toes.

While I was getting excited by where I was, and watching my wife bargaining for prices for the items she wanted to buy, someone touched me softly on my shoulders. "Who might it be?" I murmured to myself. It took me a while before I looked back to see who touched me.

"You might be from the States," said a beautiful young lady with an American Accent.

"Yes..." I said.

"What are you doing in my city?" she said.

I stared at her with scrutiny. I knew for sure that she was not from here. I could not comprehend what type of a person she was. She could be white, black or an expatriate from one of the Arabian countries. Her outfit did not portray her to be either white or American.

"What's your name?" I asked.

"Dupont..." she answered with a smile. She got me wondering and confused.

"Why are you dressed like this?" I asked.

"I love it this way. Africa is the sweetest place on earth and I wish I could be one of them."

"You mean the cultural stuff? I asked.

"How can you cope with that?"

"When you want something you just have to forego your lifestyle..."

"Your name reminds me of Dupont Circle. Are you a Hippie?"

"Why? The way I dress, sort of..." Dora was busily shopping for things we would take along with us back to the States. She did not even look back to see where I was or what I was doing. The market women were just looking at us. Dupont told me a lot about herself. She was an American Jew but having lived in Ghana for some time, she wished she were a Black Jew. She even told me that I was lucky to have a Ghanaian wife because of their cultural restrictions.

"I wish I could do that, at least to find me a date among them, but my husband, a conservative Jewish, calls me every day of the week asking me to come home."

"You are kidding me. Your husband is ten thousand miles away and he is still controlling you from there? You might be the most honest wife in the universe?" I said.

"It's not easy for me, a white lady to date a black person, an African per se. My people will kill me if they find out."

"I still don't believe you. I know you sneak sometimes," I assumed. She just laughed. Before I could say anything, my wife appeared from nowhere to get more money from me. When she saw me conversing to the white lady she looked at her up and down and winked her eyes at me. She did not ask who she was.

"My name is Dupont from the States," she introduced herself to Dora anyway.

"It's nice to meet you. I mistook you to be somebody else," retorted my wife.

"I was just telling him how lucky he is to marry an Ashanti lady, especially an educated and beautiful person like you," she commented. My wife turned around and asked me if I heard what Dupont said. She did not have to tell me anything more for I knew where the two ladies were coming from.

"My presence in Ghana will change all that." I said. At this time my wife held my hand and we moved away to the jewelry department.

In this section I found out that some traders were posing as bankers. There were three consecutive shelves and the owners were changing foreign currencies into the local currency and vice versa. To my surprise, my wife changed some of the local currency we had into the American dollars ($300). I was greatly marveled about this business. The people, I learned later, that they were illiterates. They handled cash in such an open marketplace with no police or security presence. When the money changer found out that we came from the States, he delayed us with his jovial conversation about foreigners. While we were still with him, another customer came in to change $350 into the local currency. I asked the man why the people did not go to the bank.

"My friend, I do better business with my customers than the bank. They call our business "Black Market" but the customers come here because we give them more local money for the foreign currencies than what the banks offer them," he replied in broken English.

"That makes sense. Where do they keep this money after business ... " I murmured to my self.

"We have to go," said Dora.

When we came out from the shelf, we ran into Mrs. Dupont again. I could not wait to ask about how she thought about people exchanging money in the open market without worrying about being robbed. She stared at me and smiled.

"Your wife needs to tell you more about her people and their culture. This means that Africa is a different world. That's the beauty about this place."

"You mean nobody will rob them?" She laughed. At the same time my wife joined us from the opposite booth where she had bought some gold earrings and necklace. She was curious to know what was so funny. Mrs. Dupont told her what I said. She smiled for a short while.

"He has many things to learn about Africa," she said. She looked at me in my eyes and warned me. "Never attempt to steal anything. Even though you see no police here but the people can take the law into their own hands. If you are caught stealing, you would be beaten to death before the police even arrive if they come at all."

"... and be reminded that nobody, not even the police, carry guns in this place. The culture is more fearful than the gun." My wife then stopped her, for some reason.

"Don't put any fears in my husband. Whatever he needed to know I have told him." Having said that Dora said goodbye to Mrs. Dupont, and we walked away. My whole system was filled with curiosity and I concluded that Africa is a complex place. It will take me many decades to understand it.

From the market I found myself in the midst of congested pedestrian traffic. It was like after the end of a basketball game and everybody was rushing out of the gates. You could not walk in this city without touching or running into someone. They don't even care if you touch them. That sex mania feeling is totally absent in this society. We managed to walk up the hill to a section of the city called Adum. It was like a tug of war to walk up the street. Pedestrians, vendors and the vehicular traffic were all crowded on the streets without sidewalks. Everybody seemed to have a right of way. They all seemed to be using the same public access and space. There were neither traffic lights nor marked pedestrian crosswalks to ease the traffic congestion. The motorists forced their ways through the pedestrians and vice versa. There was no traffic plan to direct anybody.

"Be careful these cars have no insurance," my wife warned me.

"...something must be done about this. Don't you have a city council?" I wondered.

"You want to go there and tell them? Maybe they will listen to you...."

Her answer was senseless to me but I could not comment on it.

Adum was part of the city, up on the hill overlooking the Subin Valley, which separates the market from the Adum downtown shopping area. Since Adum was on a hill, it provided a good view of the entire market from above and the railway lines truncating through the valley. All the major stores were at Adum. I was dazed to observe that most of the store owners were foreigners; Asians, Lebanese, Chinese, Indians, Koreans and a few natives happily traded with the people.

"Where is Black America? It should be my duty to bring them here also," I imagined. That was my dream. I just had to stop worrying to concentrate on what my wife was buying before we ran out of money. She bought something for almost everybody in my family. I had to thank her for that. I became too tired to walk so I wanted to go home.

"Man, we have not even started the sight seeing yet. This is nothing. You need to see the cultural city," she said.

"I just can't continue . . . may.be next time," I said. "I have seen enough with Kumi. It was then that she mentioned that we had to visit the cultural center, the zoo, the hospital and the King's Palace. I am yet to visit the zoo and the Cultural Center but I am tired already

"Coming to Kumasi without visiting the cultural center is like drinking a coffee without sugar," remarked Dora.

Whatever she said I won the debate with the consensus that next time we return to Kumasi. We would visit those places.

"When you were in America, you considered yourself like a champion. Now see how you are behaving like a baby. You can't even walk," she rebuked me while we were going home in a Taxi. The taxi driver laughed and joked.

"You married him to make him stronger. You must encourage him to visit very often to learn more."

We arrived home and all the children came outside to help us to carry the stuff home. Now we have only two days to leave the country.

We asked for permission to come to the capital to see to our traveling arrangements. The family bid us farewell with pomp. Our time was so short that I did not want to travel by road. We flew from Kumasi to Accra via the Ghana Airways.

The family, including Mary's co-staff saw us off on May 15, 1980 on our flight back to the sweet United States. Mary was proud of me as her Afro-American brother who had come home to roost in his roots.

On the contrarily, upon our arrival, my wife revealed that she was two months pregnant. I was filled with joy and excitement but innately I began to worry about my crazy ass unpredictable Yolanda. I just had to avoid her as much as I can.

The End

www.ingramcontent.com/pod-product-compliance
Lightning Source LLC
LaVergne TN
LVHW091554060526
838200LV00036B/831